Tom Murphy

The Mommo Plays

Brigit
Bailegangaire
A Thief of a Christmas

Tom Murphy was born in Tuam, County Galway. He lives in
Dublin. He has received numerous theatre awards and holds
honorary degrees from Trinity College Dublin and the
National University of Ireland, Galway. In 2013 he was
awarded the Ulysses Medal by University College Dublin.
He appeared on an Irish postage stamp in 2009. A six-play
season celebrating his work – Tom Murphy at the Abbey –
was presented at the Abbey Theatre in 2001. In 2012 a cycle
of his plays was produced by Druid, which played in Galway,
Dublin, London, Oxford, New York and Washington. He
has written for television and film, and a novel, *The Seduction
of Morality*. His stage plays include *On the Outside* (with Noel
O'Donoghue), *A Whistle in the Dark*, *A Crucial Week in the Life
of a Grocer's Assistant*, *Famine*, *The Morning After Optimism*, *The
White House*, *On the Inside*, *The Sanctuary Lamp*, *Epitaph Under
Ether* (a compilation from the works of J.M. Synge), *The Blue
Macushla*, *Conversations on a Homecoming*, *The Gigli Concert*,
Bailegangaire, *A Thief of a Christmas*, *Too Late for Logic*, *The
Patriot Game*, *The Vicar of Wakefield*, also published under the
title *She Stoops to Folly* (from *The Vicar of Wakefield* by Oliver
Goldsmith), *The Wake*, *The House*, *The Drunkard* (published by
Carysfort Press), *The Cherry Orchard* (a version), *Alice Trilogy*
and *The Informer* (from the novel by Liam O'Flaherty). *The
Mommo Plays* is the eighth volume of his plays published by
Methuen Drama.

T0347920

by the same author

PLAYS: 1
(Famine, The Patriot Game, The Blue Macushla)

PLAYS: 2
(Conversations on a Homecoming,
Bailegangaire, A Thief of a Christmas)

PLAYS: 3
(The Morning After Optimism,
The Sanctuary Lamp, The Gigli Concert)

PLAYS: 4
(A Whistle in the Dark,
A Crucial Week in the Life of a Grocer's Assistant,
On the Outside, On the Inside)

PLAYS: 5
(Too Late for Logic, The Wake,
The House, Alice Trilogy)

PLAYS: 6
(The Vicar of Wakefield, The Cherry Orchard,
The Drunkard, The Last Days of a Reluctant Tyrant)

DRUIDMURPHY: PLAYS BY TOM MURPHY
(Conversations on a Homecoming, A Whistle
in the Dark, Famine)

Tom Murphy

The Mommo Plays

Brigit
Bailegangaire
A Thief of a Christmas

B L O O M S B U R Y
LONDON • NEW DELHI • NEW YORK • SYDNEY

Bloomsbury Methuen Drama

An imprint of Bloomsbury Publishing Plc

50 Bedford Square	1385 Broadway
London	New York
WC1B 3DP	NY 10018
UK	USA

www.bloomsbury.com

**BLOOMSBURY, METHUEN DRAMA and the Diana logo
are trademarks of Bloomsbury Publishing Plc**

This collection first published by Bloomsbury Methuen Drama 2014

Brigit © Tom Murphy, 2014

Bailegangaire first published in 1986 by The Gallery Press, Dublin, Ireland.
Reprinted in a revised version in 1988 by Methuen London Ltd. Reprinted,
with revisions, in *Tom Murphy Plays: 2* in 1993 by Methuen Drama. Reprinted
with revisions in 2001 by Methuen Publishing Ltd. This edition first published
in 2014 by Bloomsbury Methuen Drama.

Copyright © 1986, 1988, 1993, 2001, 2014 by Tom Murphy

A Thief of a Christmas first published in 1993 in *Tom Murphy Plays: 2* by Methuen Drama.
This edition first published in 2014 by Bloomsbury Methuen Drama.

Copyright © 1993, 2014 by Tom Murphy

Introduction copyright © Nicholas Grene, 2014

Director's Note copyright © Garry Hynes, 2014

Tom Murphy has asserted his right under the Copyright, Designs and Patents Act,
1988, to be identified as author of this work.

British Library Cataloguing-in-Publication Data

A catalogue record for this book is available from the British Library.

ISBN: PB: 978-1-4742-1810-8
ePub: 978-1-4742-1811-5
ePDF: 978-1-4742-1812-2
XML: 978-1-4742-1813-9

Library of Congress Cataloging-in-Publication Data

A catalog record for this title is available from the Library of Congress.

Typeset by Mark Heslington Ltd, Scarborough, North Yorkshire

jetadorejane

Contents

Introduction: the full story

It is 1984. The senile Mommo sits up in bed telling a story to her imaginary grandchildren. It is a richly ornamented folk tale of a laughing contest of long ago, but a story with such a terrible outcome that Mommo can never bring herself to finish it nor to own that the protagonists, the Stranger and the Stranger's Wife, were her husband and herself. The two now all but middle-aged granddaughters who look after her have heard the endless narrative so often they know it off by heart. They have problems of their own: Dolly, the younger, grass widow in a loveless marriage to an absent migrant worker who abuses her on his yearly holiday visits; the resident carer Mary, who has come back from a successful nursing career in England to re-find her identity in home and family, but is treated with hostile non-recognition by her grandmother. As the audience of *Bailegangaire* we listen mesmerised to Mommo's story and, as the play goes on, we (like Mary) will her on to finish it, knowing that somehow this completion will bring closure to the whole tragic, tormented life of the family.

Bailegangaire, that intimate chamber trio, is re-scored for full orchestra in *A Thief of a Christmas*. Here we flash back to the 'actuality' of how the village of Bochtán (the poor person) came by its later appellation Bailegangaire (the town without laughter). This is a Brueghel-like carnival scene, with the people in the local pub facing a miserable 'thief of a Christmas' because of a disastrous market, turning the bizarre event of the laughing contest into a black festival. According to the chronology of the ages of the grandchildren, the action of *Thief* would be thirty years before *Bailegangaire*, therefore in the 1950s. But the stage direction describing the onstage audience of the laughers suggests a deprived Irish rural community from even more remote periods. These are people 'shaped and formed by poverty and hardship. Rags of clothing, deformities.' We are reminded of the horrors so vividly dramatised in Murphy's extraordinary play *Famine* about the great disaster of mid-nineteenth-century Irish history. And sure enough, one of the first topics raised, when the contestants are agreed on the subject of 'misfortunes' for laughing matter, is the failure of the potato crop. As the Stranger, Séamus O'Toole, laughs it out against the big-bellied local champion Séamus Costello, both private traumas and shared sorrows are given public voice: the tragic accidents and bereavements that have left Mommo and Séamus sole guardians of their grandchildren, the deprivations of the poor people of Bochtán that keep them always on the edge of starvation. It is a ritual exorcism of defiance and despair, which can have no good conclusion as the pent-up frustrated energies of the group spiral out of control.

Yet in the midst of all this chaos, Mommo and Séamus achieve a rare and lovely moment of togetherness. The back story of that relationship emerges in *Brigit*: the stand-off between Séamus, in revolt against the Church which has failed to pay him for carpentry work, and Mommo, conventionally devout, who has to sneak the grandchildren out the back way to Mass. The parish priest attempts to mollify the anti-clerical Séamus by getting him the commission to make a statue of St Brigid for a local order of nuns. The creation of this statue becomes Séamus's obsession through the play, as he carves it from native bog oak. Here we are taken back to the earliest phase of Irish history, as St Brigid, together with Patrick, one of Ireland's patron saints, is reputed to be a Christian appropriation of the Celtic goddess Brigit. Séamus struggles to express in his sculpture both the pagan deity associated with the onset of spring who presides over poetry, and the self-denying, willfully celibate nun, founder of the church of Kildare. Kildare, in Irish Cill Dara, means the church of the oak, and that is what makes the ancient piece of bog oak the fitting medium for the statue of Brigid. Séamus is so outraged by the nuns' insistence that he paint over the wood, which is for him so significant of the saint's origins, that he takes it home and threatens to burn it. It is only saved from the fire by an appeal from Mommo, whose own name is Brigid, 'though so long it's been since anyone called me by first name, I've near forgot it myself'.

Bailegangaire and *A Thief of a Christmas* were written as companion plays, both originally produced in 1985. Now with the addition of the prequel *Brigit*, which itself had an earlier life as a television play, the sequence has become a triptych. Lines, incidents, references echo across the three plays. When in *Bailegangaire* Mommo growls 'An' the church owed him money', it appears a random grievance surfacing out of nowhere; *Brigit* supplies the explanation. In *Brigit* we can have no idea just why Séamus and Mommo should be sole custodians of their young grandchildren; the revelations about the missing generation of the parents of Mary, Dolly and Tom come in the other two plays. The lovely Catholic prayer *Salve Regina*, 'Hail Holy Queen', sounds through *Brigit* as Mommo schools the children in the religion forbidden to them by their grandfather, and it is given an extraordinarily moving reprise in the conclusion of *Bailegangaire*. Naming is extremely important throughout the three plays, naming and the failure to name: Mommo cannot bring herself to accept that she was the Stranger's Wife of her story, and it is as the Stranger's Wife that she is known throughout *Thief*. Mommo itself is just the children's Irish word for Granny. She and her husband are so lost in their functions as breadwinner and housewife that their individual identities are suppressed. The rare moments when Mommo is called Brigit, when she can remember 'poor Séamus', and finally recognise her granddaughter Mary are all the more poignant as a result. As *The Mommo Plays*, the sequence highlights in particular the distorted roles of women in Ireland, whether canonised as St Brigid, allegorised as Cathleen ni Houlihan, or reduced to matriarch and domestic caregiver.

This is the story of a marriage, a family, a society, a culture – now you have it, the full story.

Nicholas Grene
July 2014

Acknowledgements

For help with these plays I am indebted to the Folklore Department, UCD, Dr Bairbre Ní Fhloinn in particular. Thanks to: Seán Ó Dúinn OSB for permission to quote (in Brigit) some lines from his book *The Rites of Brigid: Goddess and Saint*; Anne O'Reilly, Celtic scholar, and Jane Brennan for supplying me with research material; Thomas Conway, Literary Manager of Druid, for preparing the scripts for publication; and the Abbey Theatre – thanks again – this time through Ruth McGowan and Jessica Traynor.

To Tony O'Malley, RHA, who gave me, in the mid-1960s, the true story of the statue, the handyman and the bog oak, and to Frank Hugh O'Donnell – a playwright, among other things – who gave me the true story in 1971 of a laughing contest that happened near my home town earlyish in the twentieth century.

Tom Murphy

Tom Murphy

Brigit

Brigit was first performed by Druid in Galway on the 9th of September 2014 with the following cast:

Séamus	Bosco Hogan
Mommo	Marie Mullen
Mary	Lily McBride (Galway)
	Sarah Conway (Dublin)
Dolly	Ailbhe Birkett (Galway)
	Susie Power (Dublin)
Tom	Colm Conneely (Galway)
	Joshua Lyons (Dublin)
Father Kilgariff	Marty Rea
Reverend Mother	Jane Brennan
Young Nun/Old Nun	Rachel O'Byrne

Directed by	Garry Hynes
Set & Costume by	Francis O'Connor
Lighting by	Rick Fisher
Sound by	Gregory Clarke

Characters

Séamus
Mommo
Mary, *grandchild*
Dolly, *grandchild*
Tom, *grandchild*
Father Kilgariff
Reverend Mother
Young Nun, *non-speaking*
Old Nun, *non-speaking*

Scene One

1950s. A sunny Sunday morning.

The middle room – the kitchen – of a traditional three-roomed cottage. Nothing of luxury. There is an open loft across the kitchen or across a corner of it, accessed by a ladder.

The house is set back a few steps from the road. (There is nothing that could be considered as a front garden. There is no front gate or fence; a small apron of grass.)

Mommo, *aproaching sixty (?), is boiling an egg, appears to be watchful, vigilant of something.*

Séamus, *middle sixties (?), comes out of the room (a bedroom), right, picks up a chair, which he sets outside (what is meant to be) the front door, returns to the house to produce a cushion/pillow from somewhere, which he brings outside to place on the chair. Then he sits in the chair. While he is doing this, a man on a creaking bicycle passes the house.*

Man's Voice   Grand morning, Séamus, lovely morning!

Séamus   Tis! Yes.

Man's Voice (*fading*)   Tis, tis now, tis indeed!

At first it might appear that **Séamus** *has come out to luxuriate in the sunshine, but there is a set to the jaws, the neck is craned, pride/defiance in the eyes and he is not very interested in passers-by by his tone of voice. His boots are unlaced, waistcoat unbuttoned, collarless shirt open at the neck.*

While this is going on, **Mommo** *is taking her opportunity, something secretive about her and what she is carrying (children's coats), crosses the kitchen and goes into the room, left (children's bedroom).*

Another man on a creaking bicycle passing by.

Another Man's Voice   Grand morning, Séamus!

Séamus   Yes! Grand!

And Another Man's Voice   Grand morning, Séamus!

Séamus　Yes! Yes!

Voice (*fading*)　Grand, grand . . .!

Door to bedroom, left, opens and **Mommo** *comes out, cautiously. She whispers an instruction:*

Mommo　Come on.

Three children come out of the room. They are **Dolly***, aged nine* (?)*,* **Tom***, six* (?) *and* **Mary***, a demure twelve* (?)*. They are dressed in their Sunday best, which is not of high degree.* **Tom** *is towing a homemade toy, a wooden horse with a well-carved head, perhaps with wheels on the end of the legs. They are stepping carefully,* **Mommo***'s eyes on the door outside of which* **Séamus** *is sitting.*

Other voices, passers-by, calling morning greetings to **Séamus***, if required.*

Mommo *gives a prayer-book to* **Mary***, another one to* **Dolly** *and rosary beads to* **Tom***, and then whispers:*

Mommo　Off with ye now.

Tom *relieves himself of the wooden horse, sends it careering across the floor, with a yelp:*

Tom　Giddy up!

Mommo*'s shock, alarm. But* **Séamus** *does not register* **Tom***'s action or voice; he is checking his fob watch as for some synchronisation.* **Mommo***'s finger to her lips for the utmost caution and silence; and* **Tom** *saying it for her:*

Tom　Shhh!

And in exaggerated tiptoes he goes out (*what is meant to be*) *the back door, following* **Mary** *and* **Dolly***.*

A family on the road, passing by: voices of 1) man, 2) wife and 3) daughter, in chorus:

> Séamus!
> Nice morning!
> Grand morning!
> Morning! (*Daughter*)

Séamus   Tis!

Mommo (*as if the children were still in the house*)   Go out with ye now and play in the sunshine! (*And she is unsure what to do next.*)

Woman's Voice   It's a good morning, Séamus?

Séamus   It is, a good morning, Winnie.

Woman's Voice   The weather has settled?

Séamus   It has, Winnie.

Woman's Voice   It surely has, thanks be to God . . .

Mommo *is joining him in the front door; she looks after the woman who has just passed by.*

Mommo The long-faced widow Winnie. Come in: the egg I boiled for your breakfast is on the table.

He's ignoring her, checking the fob watch again.

And the water is boiled in the kettle if you'd care to wash and shave . . . What use is it every Sunday morning sitting out here waiting for the –

Séamus   *Chitch!* ('Shhhh!')

He is reacting to a bicycle approaching.

Mommo (*very gruffly*)   Come in, will you!

She withdraws to the kitchen quickly, to hide her shame. **Séamus** *stretches his legs, puts his hands behind his head to affect greater pretence of casualness.*

The bicycle is passing the house.

Father Kilgariff's Voice (*self-consciously*)   Morning Séamus!

Séamus   Good morning, your dear reverence!

Now that **Father Kilgariff** *is gone,* **Séamus** *rises and, his job done, he returns the chair and cushion to the house. The cushion, perhaps, is a pillow and he returns it to the bedroom.*

Mommo   Sit in to your breakfast.

He returns from the bedroom.

Séamus (*mock casually*)   Where are the children?

Mommo   Out the back, sure. Playing in the sunshine.

Séamus *cocks his ear for the sound of children at play.*

Mommo   They're down the fields.

Séamus (*his ear cocked again*)   Where?

Mommo   Down (in) the back field.

The church bell starts to ring the five-minute warning for Mass.

Séamus   I'm not speaking to you!

And he sits at the table to his boiled egg.

Scene Two

Convent chapel.

A light up on a **Young Nun**. *She is still in her teens, hunched shoulders, sniffling, a duster in her hands, somewhere near a niche/ alcove, empty of adornment. Beneath the niche, the fragments of a broken statue.*

Reverend Mother *and* **Father Kilgariff** *come in. She is fiftyish, a bit of an air about her, a bit affected, a bit neurotic, a bit hawk- eyed, a bit of a lisp, perhaps, and given to using French words and phrases, middle class. He is an unaffected, easy-going man; women are the bane of his life. He is about the same age as* **Séamus**.

Reverend Mother   That was a nice Mass this morning and, if you don't mind my saying it, better than your usual.

Father Kilgariff   I try to do my best.

Reverend Mother   We have a problem over here. (*To herself.*) Problems.

He starts to puff a tuneless whistle.

Reverend Mother (*indicating the broken statue*)   What do you think of that?

Father Kilgariff   It's broken.

Reverend Mother (*at the* **Young Nun**)   Tck, *disgracieux*! (*To* **Father Kilgariff**.) Yes?

Father Kilgariff   There's no way that can be mended.

Reverend Mother (*at the* **Young Nun**)   *Gaucherie! Malhabile!*

Father Kilgariff   Smithereens. Chalk. (*Meaning the statue was made of chalk.*)

Reverend Mother   Chalk, plaster, what you will – (*To* **Young Nun**) Stop your whingeing or I'll give you a skelp! (*To* **Father Kilgariff**.) That's St Brigid. We have, needless to say, a particular devotion to her. What are we to do?

Father Kilgariff   Couldn't ye buy another one?

Reverend Mother   Of St Brigid! Oh run along you – you – postulant! It's the last time you'll see chapel duty: I'll find the fitting work for your talents!

Young Nun *hurries from the chapel, tearfully, with her duster.*

Reverend Mother   When have you seen a statue of St Brigid in a shop? Or a picture! It's hard enough to get St Patrick, our patron saint. The others, yes. (*Then a sudden, high-pitched, derisive laugh.*) Italians! But there you have it again, our own, our two top saints and you'd walk the shops of Dublin without finding either one of them – What?

Father Kilgariff *nods solemnly.*

Reverend Mother   Is that propitious?

Father Kilgariff   It's a strange thing, right enough.

Reverend Mother   Inspiriting? Salutory, auspicious? Supportive . . . *Scandaleux*!

Father Kilgariff *is nodding wisely.*

Reverend Mother   So what are we to do?

Father Kilgariff *is whistling tunelessly again.*

Reverend Mother   Then will you please, *please*, communicate the problem to the bishop and the extent of our distress.

Father Kilgariff   A-a-aw! (*A degree of alarm.*)

Reverend Mother (*her alarm at his alarm*)   What-what?!

Father Kilgariff   The bishop has a lot on his plate.

Reverend Mother   A lot on his? Father, do you not think something *ought* to be done for us? We sisters – women – are alas dependent. We too try to do our best.

He screws up his eyes, heavenward: the expression that begins in frustration ends in inspiration.

Father Kilgariff   I wonder could we get one made?

Her hawk-like, though doubtful, eyes are on him.

Father Kilgariff   I think I have the man for you.

Scene Three

The kitchen is vacant of anyone. Then a creaking bicycle is approaching. The creaking stops. Then a shadow falls across the doorway and **Father Kilgariff** *arrives to stand in the doorway. He is nervous and unsure.*

Then **Mommo** *comes through the back doorway – with a sheet from the clothes line. She is always working.*

Father Kilgariff   Ma'am!

Mommo   Father!

Father Kilgariff   I see the children out there, across the wall: the stretch (is) coming into their limbs?

Mommo   Yes. (*Or she bows.*)

Father Kilgariff   Is himself in?

Mommo *goes to the room, right.*

Tom *has come in from the yard, also, and he goes to his toy wooden horse.*

Father Kilgariff   How's the man! That's a grand little – What is it? A horse you have there, is it?

Tom   Horse.

Father Kilgariff   Horse, mmmmh! And was it your grandad made that for you? (**Tom** *nods.*) And what do you call your little horse?

Tom   Horsey.

Father Kilgariff   Not a bad name at all for him.

Séamus *comes in – a book in his hand by his side – followed by* **Mommo**.

Father Kilgariff   Grand day, Séamus!

Séamus   It is.

Mommo   Run out and play, Tom, the gander won't go near you.

Tom *goes outside.*

Mommo   Won't you sit down, Father?

Father Kilgariff   No, I'll, well, for a minute. If that's alright?

Mommo   A cup of tea?

Father Kilgariff   No! No tea, ma'am. I'm poisoned with it, wherever I go!

Mommo *goes out the back door.* **Séamus** *remains standing, whatever* **Father Kilgariff** *does.*

Father Kilgariff   That's a grand flock of geese you have out there, Séamus. Tom Dineen's flock is nearly as big, and as for the Cullinanes, the swarm in their yard!

Séamus   Did you want to buy a few of them, are you just visiting, or did you come with the rest of the money you owe me?

Father Kilgariff   A-a-aw! I came about a few matters, as a matter of fact, Séamus.

Séamus   Two weeks' work, two pounds a week, what does that come to?

Father Kilgariff   Séamus, we've had this out before.

Séamus   And we'll have it out again! Two weeks work, two pounds a week and you gave me three.

Father Kilgariff   But listen to me –

Séamus   And I was waiting three months for that!

Father Kilgariff   But how am I to explain to the bishop them few jobs in the church would go on for two weeks?

Séamus   Was I sitting down doing them? – Or kneeling either?

Father Kilgariff   But do you not recall the other jobs had to be done in the church at the time – the pane in the stain-glass that went on us and the fee –

Séamus   Did I break it?

Father Kilgariff   And the fee of the expert that came over from –

Séamus   I don't recall the fee or the expert – wherever he came from – I couldn't care less! – but I recall the blacksmith over in the village, a craftsman, Joe Connealy, still waiting on his death bed, a dying man, for his pay – for his *fee* – from you or your boss, the bishop, for the iron railings he made for you. Iron scroll-work!

Father Kilgariff   Aw now, fair is fair: That was –

Séamus   Fair is fair – skilled work from Joe, tricky work from myself, mending them broken pews, chasing motifs on ends of two of them for you and that fretwork was gone in the confessional.

Father Kilgariff   But how are we to have money for everything?

Séamus   You don't need money: you don't pay anyone!

Father Kilgariff   Aw, fair is fair: How am I to stand up Sunday after Sunday asking my flock for money, how am I to deal with notifications by the dozen from the bishop instructing me to be looking for money, how am I expected to have put aside money for – (*He gestures towards* **Séamus**.) – for the little emergencies?

Séamus   That's your business.

Father Kilgariff   And the same bishop – (*He stops himself with a heavy sigh at the thought of the bishop.*) . . . People are born tight.

Séamus   All I know about the man is that he lives in a palace.

Father Kilgariff   All right. Will you tell me this: Do you consider it's right trying to keep the children, playing out there, away from the house of God on a Sunday?

Séamus   Is this the purpose of your visit?

Father Kilgariff   Will you tell me that?

Séamus   They're my grandchildren!

Father Kilgariff   Aw-haw! You'd keep children – three orphans – away from the house of God because of a –

Séamus   They're my –

Father Kilgariff   Because of the difference of a pound between us, because of a trifle.

Séamus   Pay me the trifle (then)!

Father Kilgariff   G'wan outa that! Three innocents! What you do is one thing, but to try to keep children – orphans – away from the church, the house of God of a Sunday, why, I'd almost call it diabolical.

Séamus   The house of, the house of? – You're not standing in the house of God now: *my* house!

Father Kilgariff   *Skelong* ('Get along') outa that, yeh know it isn't right, you haven't a leg to stand on!

Séamus   Is this the business you're here on?

Father Kilgariff   It isn't. But I wanted to bring it up. The whole country laughing at you.

Séamus   *What* is your business here, your reverence?

Father Kilgariff   Well . . . (*He takes a deep breath.*) I have another job for you. Don't be looking at me like that, it's not for me.

Séamus   Work for who?

Father Kilgariff   For the nuns. (*He closes his eyes.*) For the good sisters above in the convent. Will you listen to me, will you, and let me finish?

Séamus *hasn't said a word.*

Father Kilgariff   It's a commission. It's a, it's a special kinda job, a commission, a commission for a *statcha* ('statue'), a statcha, a statcha of St Brigid: The one they had was broken, smithereens – it was only chalk – I saw it myself – being dusted by, by a clumsy postulant, the Rev Mother called her: And other things in French, I think. But she, the Rev Mother, will see that she – the postulant – will never see chapel duty again and will find work more suitable for her talents – the laundry, I dare say. A statcha – are you listening to me? All knowing the great pair of hands you have: I'm putting it your way – to make it out of whatever you like – carve one or whatever – look at the little horse over there – 'Horsey'. I know things are bad for everyone, there's no work going and I thought I'd do you the turn . . . It's nothing whatsoever to do with me, Séamus, you'd have to talk to herself, the Rev Mother, about it and she's – she's – she's a decent, a decent woman enough. And measure the place, the niche, the cavity in the wall, where the statcha stood, and make your own arrangements with her. So suit yourself, Séamus, make up your own mind, but I'm in trouble again, now, with my housekeeper, Mrs Kemple. Mrs Kemple (*He shuts his eyes at the thought of the dinner on the table and the housekeeper.*) The dinner on the table for three-quarters of an hour for me, talking to you.

Scene Four

An oil-lamp lights the three children who are sitting at the table in the kitchen. (The oil-lamp lights them 'up'?) **Mary** *is engrossed in her homework,* **Dolly** *and* **Tom** *are taking their supper (porridge or some simple fare), giggling and trying to kick each other under the table.*

Mommo *is on one side of the fire, mending children's clothes.* **Séamus** *is seated on the other side of the fire, trying to think, contemplating the 'commission', and remembering past experiences of working for the clergy, distrustful of further dealings with them, male or female.*

His thoughts interrupted:

Séamus   Stop, Tom!

And, after a moment:

Mommo   Dolly! Stop your trick acting there now: Finish your supper, it's time for bed.

Séamus *rises, head bowed, just stands there, sighs and completely absently, on another sigh:*

Séamus   Stop, Tom.

And after a moment, he sits again and looks at the fire.

Mommo   Finish up now, put the books away, Mary, and take the candle.

Séamus *rises again, contemplates the floor and, after a moment, paces the length of the kitchen, while* **Mary** *is tidying away her books.* **Séamus** *paces back to the fire again, considers the fire, considers the floor, then, rather suddenly, his eyes dart to the loft and hold on the loft a few moments. But then – to the floor? – to himself – and not quite distinguishable:*

Séamus   Can you trust them?

Mommo *is, of course, aware of* **Séamus**'s '*agitation' and is putting away the clothes she was mending.* **Mary** *has tidied her books away and is taking the crockery off the table to put it away.*

Mommo   Light the candle, Mary.

Mary *lights the candle in its candle-stick and, on* **Mommo**'s *remark, leads the procession into the bedroom, left.*

Mommo   Bed. Come on now, my fondlings. Hail, Holy Queen – Yes?

Children (*as they go to the bedroom*)   Hail, Holy Queen, Mother of Mercy.

As **Mommo** *is following the children into their bedroom,* **Séamus** *is going out the back door.*

Mommo (*following the children off*)   Hail our lives – Yes?

Children (*off*)   Hail our lives, our sweetness and our hope.

Mommo (*off*)   To thee do we cry?

Children (*off*)   To thee do we cry, poor banished children of Eve.

Séamus *is returning in back door with a ladder, which he props against the loft and starts to climb. Through the following, he is leaning into the loft – moving pieces of bric-à-brac aside . . .*

Mommo (*returning to the kitchen, going to the fire, and, as said, aware of* **Séamus**'s *movements*)   Poor banished children of Eve. To thee do we send up our sighs – Yes?

Children (*off*)   To thee do we send up our sighs –

Mommo *and* **Children**   Mourning and weeping in this valley of tears.

Mommo *removes a cast-iron lid of a pot from the hot ashes or the coals of the fire and slips it into a knitted woollen cover – a bed-warmer – and takes it to the children's room.*

Mommo   Turn then, most gracious advocate, thine eyes of mercy towards us –

Children (*off*)   Turn then, most gracious advocate, thine eyes of mercy towards us –

Mommo (*off*)   And after this our exile? –

Children (*off*)   And after this our exile show unto us the blessed fruit of thy womb Jesus.

Mommo *and* **Children** (*off*)   O clement, O loving, O sweet Virgin Mary, pray for us who have recourse to thee.

Séamus *has found what he is looking for and is contemplating it on the top of the ladder.*

Mommo *comes out of the children's bedroom and stands outside it.*

Mommo   Think of your mammy and daddy is (who are) in heaven now, tell them ye're good and we all love them.

Séamus *is descending the ladder with the object he has found in the loft. It is a piece of bog oak, sometimes called black oak (I think) but it is really brown in colour. He takes it to the hearth and blows the dust off it, while* **Mommo** *lights a candle and goes into the bedroom, right, unloosening her hair.*

Séamus *sits by the fire, the length of bog oak across his knee. He is not looking at it but stroking it, slowly, rhythmically, with the cuff of his sleeve. (The oak is perhaps four feet in length, one foot in diameter, irregular in shape throughout.)*

He sits there, neck craned, motionless except for his stroking of the length of bog oak, now with the palm of his hand, lovingly, unconsciously, faintly smiling, by the dying embers of the fire.

Séamus   But can you trust them?

Scene Five

The convent chapel.

Reverend Motherother *is talking volubly and gesturing wildly:*

Reverend Mother   We don't know, of course, what you will come up with, but St Joseph! St Joseph down there! – Have you seen St Joseph? Well that's a very good image of him: I believe it – I've heard it with my own two ears – I believe it! – from a distinguished DD – he actually visited here, three years ago. A handsome man? – six footer? St Joseph. St Anthony? Catherine of Sienna? St Anthony's colours, the modesty, humility of colours. Very inspiring to us, all of their eyes heavenward, which we, in turn – (*She screws her eyes upwards.*) You know? . . . We don't know what you will come up with, but . . . The Little Flower?

Séamus *is measuring the niche where the statue is to stand and making a sketch of it with a stub of a pencil on a scrap of paper, and gauging it, critically.*

Reverend Mother   Christ on the cross? His wounds. My heart bleeds for him.

Séamus   What did she look like?

Reverend Mother   Who?

Séamus   Brigid.

Reverend Mother   Spiritual. Very spiritual.

Séamus   Not like you. I mean –

Reverend Mother   *Bonté divine!* (*Then her high-pitched laugh.*) Not like me! Of course! *Bonté du ciel!* – Good gracious! She was a saint! Her skull is in Portugal. Did you know that?

Séamus   But her face?

Reverend Mother   Noble.

Séamus   But down to earth.

Reverend Mother   I expect she was. She was called Mary of the Gael? And not unlike the Blessed Virgin.

Séamus   But bigger boned.

Reverend Mother   What do you mean?

Séamus   Brigid was one of our own, the Blessed Virgin was Jewish, a foreigner.

Reverend Mother   I would hardly call the mother of our Saviour a foreigner.

Séamus   But smaller. Brigid, her face. I've seen the statues of the Blessed Virgin, and I'd say she was – dainty. She would hardly raise her eyes to look at you. Brigid was a big woman I've heard it said. I used to hear the old people around the fire, that she was big-boned – stories, especially on Brideóg's Night. That she had girth.

Reverend Mother   A thousand and one things to do, Séamus. All sainthood has that noble and spiritual element and expression in common, regardless of their race or how tall they were, because, all of us, have the same purpose on earth, to do God's work.

Séamus   Yes. ('Yes, I see', *but perhaps he merely bows.*)

Reverend Mother   So if you've got all your measurements, I'll run.

Séamus   Before you do, Mother.

Reverend Mother   Yes?

Séamus   There's something we haven't settled.

Reverend Mother   Yes?

Séamus   There's something we haven't agreed on. Yeh know?

Reverend Mother   How long will it take you?

Séamus   I don't know.

Reverend Mother   What is there to settle then?

Séamus   So that we know where we stand, the two of us.

Reverend Mother   How much?

Séamus   So that there won't be any ongoing arguments between us.

Reverend Mother   How much?

Séamus   Five pounds.

Reverend Mother   *Sacré coeur*! And you don't know how long it will take you?

Séamus   No.

Reverend Mother   And you're not even a carpenter, Séamus.

Séamus (*agrees*)   No.

Reverend Mother   Not a trained one, I believe.

Séamus   No. I'm a *gobán* (self-trained carpenter who didn't serve an apprenticeship).

Reverend Mother   You see?

Séamus   Yes.

Reverend Mother   You see?

Séamus   But.

Reverend Mother   Yes?

Séamus   You're not a farmer.

Reverend Mother   I don't follow?

Séamus   That's a fine herd of cows out there.

Reverend Mother   Yes? *Oui* –

Séamus   Well-looked after –

Reverend Mother   Yes?

Séamus   By yourself and the sisters –

Reverend Mother   Yes?

Séamus   You're not a farmer.

Reverend Mother   I'm not a? (*And, a further moment, she gets his argument.*)

Séamus   Five pounds.

Reverend Mother   *Absurdité*! Something like a pound or two, I had in mind. Things are tight. One-ten, Séamus.

Séamus (*shakes his head*)   And there'd have to be money down, a deposit.

Reverend Mother   But where would the convent be if I flung its money away?

Séamus   I don't know.

Reverend Mother   The poor sisters and myself would land up in the poor house. Or worse! The street! Do you have any idea?

Séamus   No. (*Blandly.*)

Reverend Mother   Do you know what I picked up Blessed Martin in the town for, do you?

Séamus   Buy one in the town then of Brigid.

Reverend Mother   She's not to be had! (*A bargaining mistake and she knows it.*) . . . I'll give you . . .

Séamus   Well, I have the measurements, Mother, and you can tell Father Kilgariff to call on his way home if you want me to go ahead, with a deposit.

Reverend Mother   Two and ten shillings down.

Séamus   Four ten.

Reverend Mother   Three.

Séamus   Four.

Reverend Mother   Three ten and one down as a deposit.

Séamus   Four and two down.

Reverend Mother   I'll tell you what I'll do: I'll give you –
But don't expect to be remembered in our prayers, Séamus.
(*And she sighs, dramatically, preparatory to making her final offer.*)
I'll give you – (*And she breaks into her high-pitched laughter.*)
Mère de mon divine Jesus!

And **Séamus** *smiles, politely, and laughs with her in compliment.*

Scene Six

*Lights up on the kitchen table. It has a second oil-lamp. It has neatly
laid tools upon it, including a neat line of chisels, a saw and a vice
attached to it. (It has been commandeered as a work-bench.)*

Mommo *is standing by, holding a sandstone (operated by a handle).
She looks very tired.*

Séamus *comes in, with a whetstone/oilstone and a file. He is
exuding an inner excitement, eyes dancing. He takes the sandstone
from her and attaches it to the table. (He is still conscious of 'not
speaking' to* **Mommo**.) *He calls:*

Séamus   Mary!

Mommo   Ara what!

Séamus   Come out and turn the sandstone for me!

Mommo   Sure she can't.

Séamus (*A chisel. He hardly knows who he is talking to.*)   This
won't do. This is blunt.

Mommo   How'd you get on with the Reverend Mother?

Séamus   Mary!

Mommo   She's asleep, it's twenty to twelve!

She starts to turn the handle of the sandstone and he begins sharpening a chisel.

Séamus (*of the chisel*)   This one isn't sharp enough. This wasn't used in a long time. This isn't sharp enough.

Mommo   What class of a deal did you make with the Reverend Mother?

Séamus   I'd like it to be perfect . . . Beautiful . . . The statue . . . Unbeatable . . . She isn't as cute as she thinks she is. I'd've settled for three, but I got four out of her and one down . . . I'd like it to be what I feel . . . And I don't know what that is.

He inspects the chisel that he has just sharpened and lays it down. He takes out a little purse and produces a pound from it, which, without looking at her, he lays before her.

Her silent delight.

He starts to clean up the swarf/dust from the sandstone.

Mommo   Leave that.

Séamus   No.

Mommo   No, leave that!

Séamus   No.

Mommo   I'll do it!

Séamus   No.

Mommo   No!

Séamus   No.

She goes into the bedroom, right.

He is already honing the chisels – or the chisels – honed. He starts to sing to himself:

Séamus 'Tooralloorallooraladdy, tooralloo ralloo rallee' – Has to be . . . strong . . . perfect . . . unbeatable . . . 'Tooralloorallooraladdy, toralloo ralloo rallee' . . . Unbeatable . . . 'Tooralloo ralloo . . .' Beautiful. . .

He keeps on singing the same phrase of the song. And the chisels – or the chisel – honed, he takes the saw and clamps it in the vice and sharpens the teeth of it with a file.

He's still singing 'Tooralloo ralloo raladdy' and interspersing his song with: 'Yes, has to be strong . . . beautiful, strong . . . perfect . . .', which singing and comments are probably unheard underneath the rasp of the file going across the teeth of the saw, but which shows his growing, personal involvement.

Scene Seven

Mary *is washing clothes in a bath with the aid of a washboard. The bath is placed across two chairs. She is nearly finished. She wrings out the clothes with her hands and puts them on a flat basket, puts away the washboard, takes the bath out the back door where we hear her throw the water from it into the yard; she returns for the flat basket of wet clothes and takes it to the yard, presumably to hang the clothes on a line.*

Séamus *consults the piece of paper he sketched and wrote the dimensions on of the niche in the convent chapel. And he outlines on the kitchen floor the outline of the niche with a chalk-like stone.*

Dolly *is – dreamily – watching* **Séamus** *at work. He is holding the length of bog oak in front of him vertically; he rotates it, inclines it to one side, then the other, turns it upside down – he is thinking about it and viewing it, critically; and singing:*

Séamus 'Once I loved with fond affection'. Hmmm? . . . What d'you think? . . . 'All my thoughts they were in thee'. You wouldn't know, d'yeh know . . . D'yeh know? . . .' Til a dark-haired girl deceived me' . . .

He is talking/singing to himself. Now to **Dolly***:*

Hold it for me. Hold it up . . . Up . . .

She holds it up.

Up higher . . . You wouldn't know . . . What d'you think? . . .
Is it too heavy for you? . . . (*He takes it from her.*) 'And no more
he thought of me' . . . 'Tooralloorallooralladdy'. Yes, you
wouldn't know. 'Tooralloo ralloo rallee' . . . And do you tell
me, they tell you ne'er a thing about St Brigid at school?
Well-well! 'Til a dark-haired girl . . .' A Kildare woman . . .
Dolly . . . 'deceived me'.

*He has placed the piece of bog oak in the outline of the niche on the
floor. He adjusts it, et cetera. He makes experimental marks on the
length of bog oak, deletes them and makes others, circling the bog
oak, slowly and at comparative speed. He is talking to himself,
whether he uses* **Dolly***'s name or not.*

Séamus   That won't do, Dolly . . . What? . . . It's too long,
I'm afraid . . . We'll have to cut it . . . I'm afraid we'll have to
. . . Dolly . . . cut it.

He takes up the saw. He still hesitates.

It's like taking your life into your own hands.

*He saws an end off the piece and discards it. He holds up the bog
oak and regards it.*

Brigid . . . She was a good-looking woman, whatever . . .
Striking in some sort of way . . . Yes . . . Her mother, Dolly,
was a slave. Her father, some kind of noble, yes a high-up. A
chieftain? . . . But he married her, the slave, her mother: So,
the mother must have had the looks and that's where Brigid
got hers . . . I don't think I should do any more with her
until I have an idea – *in my head* – what kind of head she had.
(*He thinks to put away the work – and perhaps he does – but his
mind is still on it.*) She shaved off her eyebrows – Did you
know that, Dolly? Oh yes! I'm thinking the men were getting
fond of her.

Then a half-idea: he picks up the off-end he discarded earlier – it might serve a purpose later in the project. (He lays it aside at some point in the following.)

Mommo *comes in/has come in at this stage, carrying two (empty) buckets. She is followed by* **Mary** *with her empty flat basket.*

Mommo   Call Tom, Mary, (from) wherever he is.

Séamus   Yes, Brigid was a Kildare woman, Dolly.

Mommo   She was not.

Mary (*calling*)   Tom!

Mommo   She was from the County Louth, born in Fochart ('Faughart') in four hundred and fifty-five. Wet the tea, Mary.

Mommo *is busy from when she comes in: She is now going to the bedroom, right, from which she will return with an 'occasional' table (in lieu of the kitchen table) which she sets for tea,* **Mary** *assisting her.* **Mommo** *is busy throughout the following, more interested in the preparations for the tea than what she is saying.* **Séamus** *feels he is in competition with her.*

Tom *comes in during the following.*

Séamus   She plied her trade in Kildare.

Mommo   She did – most of the time. Are you nearly finished over there? Her feast day is the –

Séamus   The first of February.

Mommo   First of February, first of Spring, and in the old, olden days, the first of Spring was called Imbolg. Imbolg: in the belly. New life, the days getting longer, new life from the earth, fertility: sheep, cows, the fields, mothers. 'The eternal cycle': my father had it all. The mind of that man! Pull in to the table. She was a goddess before she was a Christian saint, but as my father said, much as the standing of a saint is, 'I am not sure they were right to drop her from the footing of a goddess.'

Séamus   That's as may be, but can you tell me what she looked like, her face?

Mommo   I cannot tell you that – Pull in to the table.

Séamus   You cannot tell me that?

Mommo   What does it matter? (*It's getting abrasive between them.*)

Séamus   It matters to me. She didn't look like the others in the chapel, red, blue, up on their pedestals, rolling their eyes (upwards).

Mommo   I cannot tell you what she looked like, but I can tell you a lot more if it *aids* you building the statue, if that's what you're talking about . . . if you like?

She pauses briefly, to hear his reply. He considers her question for a moment. Then he seems to nod.

Pull in (to the table). (*And she produces a plate from somewhere, lays it on the table and declares, grandly:*) Ham!

Scene Eight

The family meal. **Séamus** *and the children sit at the table.* **Mommo** *sits aside with a cup of tea in her hand and a crust of bread, watchful and up and down, attending to their needs. They are having 'ham' with their tea, which makes it special. The topic is 'Brigid' and the stories of her are punctuated with their eating and drinking.*

Mommo   There was a man one time whose name was Ailill and he was a king. He was passing Kildare one time with one hundred horse-drawn carts of wooden posts and Brigid went to him. 'Give me a couple of these cartloads of wattles,' she said to him, 'I want to build an abbey, a refuge for young women – and maybe for older women, too, who might be unhappy at home.' Ailill refused. That was all right. Until he ordered the horses to move on. The horses' hooves were stuck to the ground. They wouldn't move a step, not for the gentlest encouragement, nor, indeed, for the other kind. 'Now,' said St Brigid, 'will you comply with my request?' What choice had Ailill but to give her what she wanted? – and maybe more, because he was impressed.

Séamus   She was renowned for her beauty.

Mommo   And she had many suitors.

Séamus   Why wasn't she trapped?

Mommo   She consecrated her virginity to God. As early as thirteen years of age her father promised her to a chieftain. But she got out of it.

Mary   Thirteen?

Dolly   Thirteen?

Mommo   Yes.

Tom *silently mouths 'Thirteen!'*

Mary   Sr Domnick told us a very rich man came to woo her: 'Go home outa that', she said to him, that she could not accept his offer because she'd promised her virginity to God.

Tom   Virginity.

Mary   'Go home outa that,' she said to him. 'Go to the woods behind your house: there you will find a beautiful maiden, more comely than I, and go to her father and everything you say will be pleasing to him.'

Mommo   And it was as she said?

Mary   Yes.

Dolly   Yes.

Séamus   She promised her virginity to God? And when they came to bury her they put her down in between St Patrick and St Columba.

Mommo   As well as being a nun and an abbess, she was a bishop.

Séamus   A bishop?!

Mommo   Yes. So many suitors calling, her father promising her to this one and that, she left home, and with seven other virgins she went to the bishop and, suitably prepared, he made the eight of them nuns. But the holy bishop, Mel was his name, wasn't content with that – he wasn't right in the head, my father said – because he took the veil off Brigid, replaced it with a cap and consecrated her a bishop.

Mary   Phuhhhh! (*Or some sort of sound to say that she is impressed.*)

Séamus *laughs.*

Mommo   She was a good bishop!

Séamus   He wasn't right in the head alright

Mommo   It was protested of course that a woman should receive Holy Orders, but bishop Mel said – whether he was right in the head or not – he'd seen a pillar of wondrous light rise from Brigid's head, even up to the ceiling.

Dolly   She could perform miracles, Grandad!

Tom   More miracles! (*He's asking for more.*)

Séamus   She could make a fox stand on his head, Tom, and the fox only too delighted to be doing it for her.

Mommo   Her father's name was Dutach, her pagan father's name was Dagda and he was the father of the Irish Gods. He owned a harp that could play three types of music: *Goltraí*. Mary?

Mary   Tears, sadness –

Dolly   Tears, sadness! (*She is trying to compete with* **Mary**.)

Mommo   *Geantraí?*

Mary   Laughter?

Dolly   Laughter!

They laugh.

Mommo   And *suantraí*.

Mary   Sleep.

Dolly *and* **Tom**   Sleep!

Mommo   Which Dagda – cute enough of him – used to befool his adversaries and send them to sleep.

Séamus   Yes, but you can't tell me what she looked like.

Mommo   (No.) But I can tell you that she was born on the eighth day of the moon, and it was upon the eighteenth day she took the veil, she was consecrated along with eight virgins and it was on the twenty-eighth day that she went to heaven. (*Exits to the room, right.*)

Dolly   More miracles, Grandad!

Séamus   Well. (*He's stuck.*) She was, she was a very hard worker. Tending the flocks of sheep, cattle, that went with the convent – that went with the abbey. She was very kind to dogs. She fed stray dogs! (*He discovers the tack he's going to go on.*) She'd be out all hours at lambing-time, on the hills at night, worn out, d'yeh know, like many a shepherd before her or since. And what did one of her ewes do but drop the lamb beside a fox hole? She had to go home, to sleep, she was so tired. But before going home she said into the fox hole, 'Well, I'm telling you now, if you harm this lamb I'll be up in the morning with Sr Jerome's two terriers and they'll deal with you.' What did she find in the morning? The poor fox running circles about the lamb, keeping the crows that were wheeling overhead away from pecking the eyes out of it.

Mommo (*returning from room, right*)   And one Holy Thursday – it was a very hot springtime, the tongues were rolling in the monks' mouths for drink – from a bag of malt she made a barrel of beer, and from that one single barrel, when the monks had drunk their fill – maybe batin' ('beating') stomps on the floor and singing comallyehs – the barrel did the rounds and satisfied eight other congregations for the eight days of Easter: a miracle!

On the last, 'a miracle', she produces from behind her back a jam roll and a bottle of lemonade.

She pours the lemonade for the children. She holds up the jam roll.

Who doesn't want some of this? . . . Who does?

Tom Me! Me!

Dolly I do! I do! Mommo!

Tom Mommo! Mommo! Mommo!

Dolly I do! I do! I do!

Mommo *slices the jam roll and, as it happens,* **Dolly** *is served first.* **Tom***'s lip is out, he's pointing towards the end piece – he wanted it.*

Tom I said it first.

Séamus Op-op-op, Tom! (*Telling him, 'Don't cry, your turn is next.'*)

Mommo (*simultaneously, of* **Tom**) Oh? The lip! (*But she serves him next.*)

It is a feast for them that they are having this evening.

Mommo (*she starts to clear away the crockery the others don't need – as in the beginning of the previous scene*) She could hang her cloak on a sun beam. She could! If it was wet or damp. Or she'd do it just for fun . . . She travelled all over, but the Leinster people wanted her back and, to tempt her, they offered her a piece of land on the edge of a grassy plain, now known to some as St Brigid's Pastures, now known to the world as the Curragh of Kildare.

Mary She built a church there under a wide oak tree.

Mommo   Since then the place has become Kill, which means?

Mary   Church –

Dolly   Church –

Mommo   Dara? –

Mary   Of the oaks –

Mommo   Cilldara: Kildare. And it became a place of pilgrimage for the lowly and forgotten, the most powerful and privileged. And now my fondlings, *suantraí*.

Dolly   Sleep!

Mary and **Dolly** *clear away the crockery, and* **Mommo** *leads them (carrying* **Tom**?*) into the bedroom.*

Mommo   O holy virgin Brigid, full of divine wisdom, shy of men, intercede with Christ our God that He may have mercy on us all.

Our attention now is on **Séamus** *who has risen and taken up a chisel; but he is hesitant.*

Dolly *comes out of her bedroom in her night clothes.*

Dolly   Grandad, I'm going to bed now.

Séamus (*To himself*)   No, I don't know, Dolly, if I should do any more with her until I have an idea, to drive me on, what she looked like. Her features.

Dolly   Grandad?

Séamus   Oh, bo, mo pheata ('my pet')! Have you a kiss for me?

She kisses him.

Off now to bed, mo chailín ('my little girl'). (*He returns his attention to his work.*)

Dolly   Grandad?

Séamus   Yes?

Dolly   Can we go to Mass on Sunday?

Séamus *glances at the room: he knows* **Mommo** *is behind* **Dolly***'s request. He nods his agreement and turns back his attention to his work.*

Dolly   Grandad? Not out the back door and across-the-fields way?

Séamus *frowns down at her, then nods his head.*

Dolly   (*smiles*) Grandad. (*Which means 'thank you and I love you'.*)

Dolly *returns to her room.*

As the lights change/fade a little (very short passage of time), **Séamus***, still with chisel in his hand and regarding the piece of oak.*

Séamus   Brigid.

Mommo *comes out of the children's room – probably for the cast-iron lid bed-warmer – letting down her hair. He regards her – the cascading hair, her head: it isn't sufficient for him. He gets his coat and goes out.*

Mommo   Where are you going this time of night?

Séamus (*off*)   Out!

Scene Nine

(*The scene is a conflation of three scenes.*)

Day.

The length of bog oak is elevated on something so that he can look up at it while he is working/chiselling away at it: **Séamus** *is earnestly and happily at work. There is celebration in what he thinks is the answer he has found to the question that was preoccupying him – 'What did she look like?' – and he is celebrating, too, where and from whom he got the answer when he was 'Out!'*

He is laughing to himself; he is a bit drunk and he is drinking from a small bottle of poitín.

Dolly *is lazily, dreamily – reclining on the floor? – watching* **Séamus** *at work.*

Séamus   What did she look like? I'll tell you. I will tell you. She had a long face. Dolly. I don't mean it was (as) long as a fiddle. But it was long . . . I don't mean it was a miserable, sorry sight, wirrasthru of a face. No. In all her humours, serious, grave, she could be – fun – too . . . Oh, I'm sure she could be, like many's another woman, sharp with you, sullen even, the way of women, times, can give you the eye (to punish you). But she was welcoming, pleasant – oh yes! – (with) laughter, mirth – oh yes! (*He laughs/chuckles in celebratory memory. He reins himself in.*) . . . As your grandmother told us the other night, all ranks and classes of people were drawn to her: people like ourselves, people of noble birth, people left their homes to seek shelter in her convents. So she must have had a balance of humours to attract uneven types . . . She had a face (that) if you came by it on the road, you'd say 'Goodday' and pass by, but it'd stay with you: it would have impressed your private notice, without maybe you even knowing it . . . Dolly . . . And if you found yourself in her company, you'd be surprised to find yourself laughing, out loud. (*He is laughing, again, as he works.*) And she was fond of a drop. I don't think it was the Lord alone made her face shine. I don't think he made it wan either. She was weather-beaten, Dolly. (*He remembers where he is, reins himself in, again.*) Well, as Mommo told us the other night, she was a dab hand at making drink. I mean, *beer* . . . Maybe she had a face (as) long as our Jostler's down the back-field paddock: I often look at him: the patience, the humility – and he does his work when called upon! – the modesty of that little horse. Times, I behold Jostler, I wonder if he isn't a saint, and if he doesn't know more than any of us . . . But yes, Brigid: She had a face you'd like to be looking upon. A face you'd see the strength of the world in, without knowing that's what you would be seeing . . .

The lights are changing from day to night. **Dolly** *leaves.* **Séamus** *continues during the transition, working.*

Séamus   Not pretty, noble or rolling her eyes. Nothing of that . . . Big face . . . Brigid.

Night.

He is now sober; working.

Mommo *has come in to sit at the fire, mending clothes, again. (Or?)*

Mommo   Her colour is white, her symbol is fire. As a goddess she was, among other things, a midwife. She was at Christ's birth. When Mary fell into bad-needed sleep, Brigit suckled Jesus. As a goddess, she was called Brigit, as a saint she was called Brigid. I don't know why that was. They took what the goddess could do and grafted it on to St Brigid's name. I don't know that that was right. The devotion to Brigit was transferred to Brigid. For 'respectability', my father said. And he wasn't pleased. She – St Brigid – slept with a young nun, always and ever the same one: She believed in a soul mate, anam cara. Her father was bent on getting her married and, yes, and so, yes, she shaved off her eyebrows, but that wasn't enough to keep them away. So what did she do? As tradition has it, she lost an eye. But she didn't lose it. She could take the eye out of her head and hold it behind her back when the suitor came wooing: So, the suitor seeing a one-eyed woman, his ardour flustered, would rattle off an excuse, and goodday or night and make his escape. And she would, to her Deliverer, with prayers of thanks, slip the eye back to where it should be. (*She collects up her things. She is very tired.*) Come on to bed outa that: You're wearing yourself out for them: Won't it be there for you in the morning? (*The lights are changing.*) And I'll teach you tomorrow all the causes she pushed and favoured. She was patroness of many things.

She has gone to bed.

The lights have faded, up and down, from night, to day to late night, **Séamus** *resolutely working all the time. He is now obsessive about his statue.*

Séamus   Patroness of babies, women in child-birth, of the hearth, fire, blacksmiths, the fields, farmers, art, stray dogs, jam, jam-making, boatmen, cattle, chickens, light, children whose parents aren't married, children with abusive fathers, children born into bad unions, milk, milkmaids, dairy workers, Leinster, fugitives, infants, Ireland . . . Ireland? Well, of course, Ireland! (*But he has thrown/distracted himself.*) . . . Leinster, fugitives, infants, Ireland . . . Ireland. Leinster, fugitives, infants . . .

Mommo's Voice (*from bedroom, right, annoyed, like one trying to sleep?*)   Leinster, fugitives, infants, Ireland, *all female concerns,* sailors!

Séamus   All female concerns, sailors, midwives, nuns, poets, poetry, the poor, hens, poultry of all kinds, printing presses, scholars, watermen, travellers, metals, metalworkers.

The lights are changing, fading up to morning. He continues resolutely working and, as in a mantra, he begins a litany, again, his voice fading as the lights grow brighter.

(Patroness) of babies, women in childbirth, of the hearth, fire, blacksmiths, the fields, farmers, art, stray dogs . . . (*His lips keep moving.*)

Scene Ten

Morning. The church bell is ringing for Mass. Light first falls on **Mommo**, *hand-in-hand with* **Tom**, *paused in the front doorway, Sunday clothes –* **Mommo** *wears a hat; she is looking back at* **Séamus** *with an expression of concern for him: his intensity frightens her.* (*His lips are moving.*)

Mary *precedes them out the door, a glance back at* **Séamus** *as she does so.*

Dolly *holds back.*

Dolly   We're going now, to Mass, Grandad? . . . Bye-bye?
. . . Bye-bye.

Séamus *works on without let-up – no acknowledgement of* **Dolly**.

Séamus   Stray dogs, jam, jam-making, boatmen, cattle,
chickens, light, children whose parents aren't married,
children with abusive . . .

Scene Eleven

*The kitchen. Lights falls on the children, returned from Mass, in a
tight group: they seem cowed, unsure/confused as to what they are
meant to do next. They are still in their Sunday clothes.*

Séamus *is working on the statue: perhaps he has it face-down on
the table, working on the back of it. (Note: From early on, from the
length/block of wood that it was, we only see the statue in its crudest
evolution; we don't see its finished form until we see it in the niche in
the convent chapel, front-on.)*

Mommo *comes in. She is very angry. She immediately starts to
upbraid the children.*

Mommo   Standing there? Standing there, standing there!
Take your good clothes off! (*To* **Dolly**.) Bring in the brishan
of turf for the fire or is that something else for me to do? –
on top of everything else! (*To* **Mary**.) Them aul books of
yours! Go down at once and throw a few turnips to Jostler,
nobody looking at that little horse of ours for almost a week
and hardly a blade of grass left in the paddock! But does
anyone notice these things? Ah, come on out of there, Dolly,
you're getting too old-fashioned altogether, always there
with your fist under your chin – Bring in the turf! (*To* **Tom**.)
And you, *mister*, with your eyes open-mouthed, go out and
drive the geese into the middle field – Run along! – You
aren't such a baby any more to be afraid of the gander.

*A bit of hectic activity: the children divesting themselves of their
Sunday clothes and obeying orders.*

Everything left for me to do and everything left after that
goes undone.

The children are gone. **Dolly** *comes in with an armful of turf
during the following and leaves again, soundlessly, diplomatically.*

Mommo *is continuous with her rant.*

Mommo   I thought we were poor like everyone else, but
did I think we were! (*To* **Séamus**.) Did you enjoy yourself the
other night when you were 'Out!'? She'll be coming over the
road for you now – from *Mass!* – your girlfriend, that you
went to see the other night when you were 'Out!'! Your
girlfriend! The whole village has it – The lanky widow with
the horse's face. Everyone had it but me: I was the blind one!
(*Going off to bedroom, right, divesting herself of her hat, coat . . .*) I
thought we were poor but did I think we were foxy, slippery,
shameless, faithless, treacherous, trickery, betrayal, rascally,
skulduggery, making a mock out of me!

*She has returned to the kitchen and she plonks herself down on the
box by the fire. She speaks doggedly, grimly, as one doing her – no
matter what – wifely duty.*

There was a blind nun in Brigid's time whose name was
Darragh. My father told me this. *He* didn't need help from
anyone. *He* had a head on him. And Darragh, the blind nun,
came to Brigid and asked her to restore her sight. Brigid
prayed and, no surprise in it, her prayers were answered.
Darragh's sight was restored. But the way the world was, full
of tricks, lies, deceit, betrayal of vows, Darragh was –
disgusted – and she came to Brigid once more and said,
'Make me blind again, make me blind, make me as I was
because the clarity of light, makes me long for the beauty of
darkness.' (*She rises.*) The clearness, the – *cleanness* – of
darkness. Cleanness! (*She has gone to the front door.*) Here she
is! Here she is! Coming to visit you, your girlfriend –
Striapach!

She vacates the doorway.

Séamus *goes to the doorway, ostensibly coolly, defiantly; and waits.
Then, he calls:*

Séamus   Goodday, Winnie! Isn't it a good day, Winnie?

Widow's Voice   It is a good day, Séamus, it is!

Séamus   It is, Winnie, it's a good day, it is!

Widow's Voice   It is, true enough! (*Fading.*) It surely is . . .

Séamus   It is, Winnie! It is! It is!

He returns to his work on the statue but his concentration is broken. And **Mommo** *is rocking herself on the box, seated by the fire.*

. . . (*To himself, sotto voce:*) Stop.

Mommo   And Father Kilgariff has it. I went to him: he had it already. He'll call on you, he said. (*She continues to rock herself on the box.*)

Séamus (*quietly*)   Stop.

She has got up and starts to prepare a mash into the buckets for the geese.

Mommo   The priest is going to call on you.

Séamus (*quietly*)   Stop. (*And because she is still whining, he, authoritatively:*) Stop!

She goes to the room, right, crying.

(*On a sigh.*) Stop.

And he sits, despairingly, unable for the moment to resume working.

Scene Twelve

Father Kilgariff *is standing in the front doorway, the light on him. He is nervous of his mission.*

Séamus *is working on the statue again and doesn't see him until he speaks. Perhaps the statue is still lying on the table, inclined to shift/ wobble on* **Séamus**.

Father Kilgariff   Can I give you a hand there?

Séamus   What brought you over?

Father Kilgariff   Just passing.

Séamus   Were you? (*Drily.*)

Father Kilgariff   I was. Can I come in? And thought I'd drop in on you to see how you were getting on.

Séamus   Is that the truth? (Is that so?)

Father Kilgariff   You're more than a week on the job now.

Séamus   Oh! her highness in the convent sent you.

Father Kilgariff   No. No. (*He starts to hold the statue, steadying it for* **Séamus**.)

Séamus   The bishop?

Father Kilgariff   No. No. (*A peace offering:*) You know we call him 'Knifeface'. The bishop.

Mommo *comes in from the bedroom, right. She glances reproachfully at* **Father Kilgariff** *that he is not doing his duty. He nods back at her and winks, broadly, shrewdly, that he is going about it.* **Mommo** *takes the buckets that she was foostering ('fussing') over earlier, and goes out with them.* **Father Kilgariff** *starts puffing a tuneless whistle. Then:*

Father Kilgariff   No but, what I wanted to say to you was –

Séamus   Hold it steady if you're holding it! . . . Knifeface.

Father Kilgariff   We call him 'Tightwad', too . . . 'Tightarse', too.

Séamus   Tightarse.

Father Kilgariff   . . . They must have clamps or some sort of vices with jaws wide enough for pieces like this to keep them steady while a man is working on them . . . But I suppose the jaws on clamps or vices would make impressions or marks on the piece.

Séamus   . . . Armatures.

Father Kilgariff   Yes?

Séamus   I'm not sure what an armature is, but I read the word: to do with sculpture.

Father Kilgariff   Oh? Yes? (*Genuinely interested.*)

Séamus   I think the word doesn't apply to work like this: solids. Or wood.

Father Kilgariff   Oh?

Séamus   Or stone.

Father Kilgariff   Yes?

Séamus   But as far as I can make it out, it's a framework, a sort of steadying structure, you have inside the piece if, say, you were working in plaster. Or wax.

Father Kilgariff   Well-well! Armatures! Wax! Well, is that so! . . . (*He takes up a carved little bird.*) What's this? What's the little bird for?

Séamus   That's a brown canary that I made for a purpose. (*He takes it from* **Father Kilgariff** *and puts it in his pocket.*)

Father Kilgariff (*a brief tuneless whistle, then:*)   Séamus. It's foolish giving rise to silly talk by calling to a woman's house late at night where there's no man in it.

Séamus *stops work for a moment to look at the floor and sigh, then resumes working again.*

Father Kilgariff   I know! I know, I know, I know, I know, I know! I know!

Séamus   Are you holding it for me?

Father Kilgariff   I am. (*He is holding/steadying the statue.*) They say the same thing about me. The stories are carried back to me – would you believe even in the confessional? – about my housekeeper, Mrs Kemple. (*He rolls his eyes to himself.*) Mrs Kemple: Would anyone, anyone, go anear her? . . . I just, Séamus, had to mention it (to you) and now it's mentioned, not another word about it. (*Puffs a relief.*)

Séamus   In the confessional.

Father Kilgariff   Yes.

Mommo *comes in, ostensibly for something; she glances at* **Father Kilgariff**. **Father Kilgariff** *winks solemnly at her that the job is done.* **Mommo** *goes out again.* **Father Kilgariff** *blows another – this time, silent – sigh of relief.*

Father Kilgariff   When will it be done?

Séamus   I don't know.

Father Kilgariff   I know. But you're nearly there.

Séamus   Yes . . . Nearly . . . Who knows?

Father Kilgariff   The pair of hands are a great man . . . I used to watch my father . . . And I was tasty enough myself one time . . . Sometimes I wonder.

Séamus   And the Reverend Mother: do you have a name for her?

Father Kilgariff   'Tighthole'.

Séamus *laughs into himself as he works.* **Father Kilgariff** *doesn't laugh. Then,* **Séamus**, *expressing a recurring doubt/worry/suspicion:*

Séamus   Will she keep her part of the bargain?

Father Kilgariff   Oh she . . . (*He doesn't know: he forgets his diplomacy, momentarily. Then:*) Oh, she will, she will. I'm sure.

Séamus *continues working.* **Father Kilgariff** *holding/steadying it for him and, as the lights fade:*

Father Kilgariff (*on a sigh*)   You will never beat the Irish church!

Scene Thirteen

Séamus *working, working, working: the statue upright, supine, slantwise. Working from evening into night, into the small hours of the morning: the lights almost imperceptibly changing to denote the passage of time.*

*At one point, a child cries in its sleep – **Tom** – as in a bad dream. As a consequence, **Mommo** is seen – not well lit – crossing the kitchen in night attire – ghostly – and going into the children's room. After a few momennts, she reappears, carrying **Tom**, to cross the kitchen again and exit to the room, right.*

Further time elapsing.

Séamus *is slowing down, the intensity of his obsession abating, giving way to humility and the quietest vindication.*

It is the small hours. (Perhaps this should be called Scene Thirteen A.) Silence all over.

Séamus *is sitting on the box beside the fire, which is nearly dead, the tears running down his face. He looks drawn, drained, (unshaven), motionless, looking across the kitchen at what only can be the finished statue. (The emotional 'incontinence' is due to the sustained, creative effort and concentration on the work over a long period of time. He is an artist.) He is just sitting there and looking, with his tears.*

Mommo *comes out of the room, right, in night attire. She comes and stands behind **Séamus**'s shoulder; she looks in the same direction that he is looking in (at the statue); then, still looking gravely at the statue, she strokes his hair, once.*

Scene Fourteen

The statue of St Brigid stands in the niche in the wall of the convent chapel – or hall. We are seeing it for the first time.

It is unlike the usual statues seen in churches. It does not have the symmetry, finish, polish or colours that are usual; it does not have the pietism, the expressions of modesty or humility that are the norm. The roughness of its hewn nature, the chisel marks, the asymmetry, the nodules on the timber are visible and are part of the strength of the figure. The face is unusually long, gaunt, even, a big-boned Irish face: bold, determined, strong; the eyes look out, un-apologetic, straight out. There is something wrong, imperceptibly to an audience perhaps, with one of its eyes. Also, there is a small bird – an attachment to one of the arms or shoulders of the statue. There is something reassuring about the whole thing, about continuity. It is a primitive, pagan, striking piece of art.

The **Reverend Mother** *is considering it: her head is inclined to one side, index and second finger on her cheek and third finger under her chin, assessing the figure. She is not a woman to be caught out, wanting in matters of art. She views it from different angles, singing, absently, 'Ten Green Bottles', in French.*

Séamus, *at some remove from her, is watching her, awaiting her verdict, and, alternatively, is looking at nothing.*

Somewhere else in the chapel/chapel hall, **Mary**, **Dolly** *and* **Tom**, *with satchels, watch and wait.* **Dolly** *is proud of her grandad and his statue,* **Tom** *is even more so, and* **Mary** *is frowning to herself at the* **Reverend Mother**'s *antics.*

Reverend Mother   *'Dix boteilles vertes s'arrêtant sur le mur . . .'* You've called at a bad time, Séamus.

Séamus   I thought you might be anxious, so.

Reverend Mother   Monday mornings.

Séamus   To see it in the niche.

Reverend Mother   *'Dix boteilles vertes . . .'*

Séamus   So I brought it over.

Reverend Mother   That was kind.

Séamus   Yes.

Reverend Mother   D'you know? (*Meaning 'Monday mornings'.*)

Séamus   Yes.

Reverend Mother   I think . . . (*She was about to give an opinion. Instead:*) *'Neuf boteilles vertes'* – Is there something wrong with one of her eyes?

Séamus   Well, everybody knows she had eye-trouble.

Reverend Mother   Oh yes, of course, of course! . . . (*A further assessment and:*) Mmmmm! '*Neuf boteilles vertes*' – (*And a further:*) Mmmmm! (*Then:*) What's the bird?

Séamus   Oh.

Reverend Mother   Did she have something about birds?

Séamus   You don't like it – the bird?

Reverend Mother   Something about St Francis?

Séamus (*concern*)   You don't like it, you don't like it?

Reverend Mother   Well, I, well, I.

Séamus   Wait a minute. There! (*He has plucked the bird off the statue.*) Is that better?

Reverend Mother   . . . '*Huit boteilles vertes s'arrêtant sur le mur . . .*'

Séamus   D'yeh think?

Reverend Mother   Mm?

Séamus   I think, I have to agree with you.

Reverend Mother   Yes?

Séamus   The bird was a late thought: an attachment that I – (*shrugs 'just'*) – fixed on. It didn't square.

Reverend Mother   It wasn't accordant.

Séamus (*puts the bird in his pocket*)   Yes.

Reverend Mother   Thank you, Séamus.

Séamus   So?

Reverend Mother   I think . . . I like it! Mmmmm! . . . But I need a second opinion. Leave it there, go home, off with you. Father Kilgariff calls for early vespers and I'll discuss it with him.

Séamus   I'll wait.

Reverend Mother   It could be five or six o'clock before he calls: there's no point in wasting your day here.

Séamus   That's all right.

Reverend Mother   It could be even later.

Séamus   I'll wait.

'Well', to him ('Suit yourself'), a final 'Mmmmm!' at the statue and leaving, 'Sept boteille vertes s'arrêtant sur le mur . . .' (etc.).

The children join him. **Dolly** *is proud of him,* **Tom** *is wagging his head from side to side in celebration, and* **Mary** *is her sober self.*

Mary   Does she like it?

Séamus   Oh, I – yes, I think she does.

Mary (*insistent*)   *Does* she, *does* she?

Séamus   There's the bell for classes.

Mary   But *what* did she say?

Séamus   Oh, she said (she said), 'it'll be all right.'

Mary   *Did* she? *Did* she?

Dolly   It'll be alright, Grandad, won't it?

Séamus   Yes. Run along with ye now to school or ye'll be late.

The bell for school has been ringing. **Dolly** *kisses* **Séamus**. **Séamus** *pats the admirative* **Tom** *on the head, produces the bird from his pocket, gives it to* **Tom** *with a wink and says, 'A brown canary', and laughs to himself about his ruse with the bird on the statue.* **Tom** *and* **Dolly** *run off.* **Mary** *remains with* **Séamus** *and they are silent for some time. (***Mary** *is privately fuming; she feels there is something wrong. She is old beyond her years in certain matters and she has a female distrust of the* **Reverend Mother**.)

Mary   . . . Tck! (*To herself.*) Cheek of her!

Séamus   . . . I think she does, Mary, like it. It's just a question of . . . she needs more time to think it out for herself.

Scene Fifteen

Convent: chapel/hall. It is evening. A clock, off, is chiming five or the half-hour (which is a single chime). The statue of St Brigid in the niche is giving out its own waiting atmosphere in the evening light.

Away from it, but watching it, in the gloom, **Séamus** *is sitting in a pew or church chair.*

Footsteps on a corridor (off) and the rustle of habits, and **Reverend Mother** *and* **Father Kilgariff** *come in, followed by an* **Old Nun** (**Young Nun** *from Scene Two doubling? – but preferably followed by a bevy of nuns).*

They regard and assess the statue, confer in whispers, assess it again and have a whispering conference . . .

Father Kilgariff *comes to* **Séamus**.

Father Kilgariff   They like it.

Séamus *nods, waits for more, two little smiles on the corners of his mouth.*

Father Kilgariff   Oh, they like it all right and I've the rest of your money here for you. (*He has the money in his hand and he is proffering it to* **Séamus**.) Three pounds and you had one down.

Séamus (*does not take the money*)   Yes? They like it – yes?

Father Kilgariff   Yes, they like it –

Séamus   Yes? –

Father Kilgariff   Yes, they do, they do –

Séamus   Yes? –

Father Kilgariff   Like it, like it –

Séamus   Yes?

Father Kilgariff   There's just one thing.

Séamus   Yes?

Father Kilgariff   They'd like you to put a drop of paint on it.

Séamus *is smiling; then, perhaps, he laughs to himself.*

Father Kilgariff   Wha'? . . . Yes?

Séamus   Yes?

Father Kilgariff   Yeh know, they were saying, a white alb sort of thing –

Séamus   Yes?

Father Kilgariff   A drop of, drop of mid-brown to the cloak and, maybe – they were saying –

Séamus   Yes? –

Father Kilgariff   Summer-green – a splash of it – on the mantle. And a drop of red – just a drop – on the. . .

Séamus *is laughing into himself.*

Father Kilgariff   What? . . . Wha'?

Séamus (*more to himself than to* **Father Kilgariff**)   Did she mention the bird?

Father Kilgariff   The bird? . . . The?

Séamus   Does she want it back, the bird?

Father Kilgariff   I don't follow.

Séamus   You dress in black, they dress in black, and you want your saints in colours?

Father Kilgariff   I've your money here.

Séamus   Have you no shame?

Father Kilgariff   I – What?

Séamus (*now overt anger*)   That's oak!

Father Kilgariff   That's oak. (*Agreeing, but he's puzzled.*)

Séamus   Bog oak!

Father Kilgariff   Bog – Yes.

Séamus   That oak is maybe older than St Brigid!

Father Kilgariff   That oak –

Séamus   Older!

Father Kilgariff   Older –

Séamus   The oak was sacred to the Druids!

Father Kilgariff   Well, maybe – Séamus, Séamus! – Maybe I can get them to change their minds.

Séamus   Other colours? Blue, sky blue, redden it?

Reverend Mother (*from afar/approaching*)   *Qu'est-ce qu'il y a?*

Father Kilgariff (*proffering it*)   Your money.

Séamus   Is there nothing sacred to ye?

Father Kilgariff   But, Séamus –

Séamus   No. (*He is going to the niche.*)

Reverend Mother   *Qu'y a-t-il? A-t-il?*

Father Kilgariff   But three pounds is three pounds!

Séamus (*to him and to her*)   Do you have respect for anything?

He takes the statue out of the niche and, carrying it under his arm, is leaving.

Father Kilgariff   But Séamus –

Reverend Mother   What? –

Séamus   No!

Reverend Mother   What is the matter?

Séamus (*to her*)   Childish!

Father Kilgariff *is positioning himself to block/impede* **Séamus's** *leaving the convent, proffering the money again.*

Father Kilgariff   Well, would you take one of these ('pound notes') to make up the difference of the pound between ourselves for the work you did in the church?

Séamus   No.

Father Kilgariff   Well, you won't take it out on the children, stop them going to Mass.

Séamus   I won't. (*Perhaps silently.*)

Séamus *is gone with the statue.*

Father Kilgariff   I'm sorry for the trouble we put you to . . .

Reverend Mother (*to herself: could she be wrong about something, anything*)   *Qu'est-ce qu'il y a?* What is the matter . . .? (*It dies on her.*)

Scene Sixteen

The kitchen table has been restored to its former use – vice and tools are gone; the statue stands on it; the occasional table (or simple dressing-table) from the bedroom, right, is still in the kitchen, somewhere.

Séamus *is seated on the box looking at nothing, but there is an anger growing in his eyes.*

Mommo *is very conscious of* **Séamus** *throughout the scene: she is concerned for him; she knows his moods and temper. She is preparing to go into the children's room with a cup of water, which she draws from a bucket. Her mind is not on what she is saying and she is glancing at him, secretly.*

Mommo   Hail Holy Queen – Yes?

Children (*off*)   Hail Holy Queen, Mother of Mercy.

Mommo   Hail our lives – Yes? (*And she goes into the children's room.*)

Children (*off*)   Hail our lives, our sweetness and our hope.

Mommo (*off*)   To thee do we cry?

Children (*off*)   To thee do we cry –

Mommo   (*re-entering; and running ahead*) Poor banished children of Eve.

Children (*off, trailing her*)   Poor banished children of Eve.

Mommo *has re-entered the kitchen, ostensibly to restore the 'occasional' table to the bedroom, right, which action is unnecessary at the moment, but which she does. (And exits again. Her movement is continuous since her re-entry and exit.)*

Séamus *now, with a deft, quick movement, tosses a sod of turf on the fire: he watches the sparks rise, then he fixes an angry glare on the statue, and mutters something indistinguishable ('What the oak meant to Brigid!')*

Mommo (*off*)   To thee do we send up our sighs?

Children (*off*)   To thee do we send up our sighs –

Mommo   (*re-entering the kitchen – from bedroom right*) Mourning and weeping in this valley of tears.

Children (*off*)   Mourning and weeping in this valley of tears.

Séamus (*simultaneously with the last*)   What the oak meant to Brigid! (*And a quick movement, another sod of turf into the fire – and the sparks rise.*)

From **Mommo**'s *return to the kitchen, she has gone to the fire to retrieve the cast-iron lid from the ashes and slips it into the woollen sleeve. Though she is at close proximity to* **Séamus**, *she is trying to behave normally.*

Séamus   What the oak meant to Brigid!

Mommo   In this valley of tears. Turn then, most gracious advocate?

Children (*off*)   Turn then, most gracious advocate –

Mommo/Children   Thine eyes of mercy towards us –

Séamus   What the oak meant to the Druids!

Mommo   And after this our exile? (*Going into the children's room.*)

Children (*off*)   And after this our exile, show unto us the fruit of thy womb, Jesus.

Séamus *throws another sod of turf into the fire; he watches the sparks rise; and laughs.*

Séamus   What the oak meant!

Mommo *comes out of the children's room, speaking simultaneously with the children, and continues across the kitchen to the bedroom, right – a fluent movement – perhaps letting down her hair.*

Mommo   O clement, O loving, O sweet Virgin Mary.

Children (*off*)   O clement, O loving, O sweet Virgin Mary.

Mommo (*as she goes into the bedroom*)   Pray for us?

Children (*off*)   Pray for us who have recourse to thee.

Séamus   Oak!

Mommo (*off*)   Holy virgin, Brigid, intercede with Christ for us now, that we may overcome our present crises.

Séamus *pokes the fire, the sparks and the flames rise; the light of anger in his eyes, he stares at the statue.*

Mommo *returns to the kitchen – ankle-length off-white nightdress, hair down – to cross the kitchen, to stand outside the children's room.*

Mommo   Think of your mammy and daddy is (who are) in heaven now, tell them you're good and that we all love them.

Séamus (*quietly, but with anger*)   And what the oak meant to Brigid!

She moves across the kitchen, head bowed: it's as if she still feigns to be unaware of him. She stops.

Mommo   Give it to me, Séamus. Don't burn it. I'm Brigit too, though so long it's been since anyone called me by first name, I've near forgot it myself.

He looks at her: the gentle smile, the sadness of life behind it, the shyness of a girl, her hair falling about her shoulders, the long white dress: it's as if he hasn't looked at her in years. He rises, slowly and, when standing, he nods, a formal bow, an acknowledgement of her.

She takes the statue and goes into the bedroom.

Séamus   Brigit.

He sits on the box, straight back, neck craned, set to his jaws, eyes bright: determination, defiance, unwillingness to submit.

The fire going down.

Tom Murphy

Bailegangaire

The story of Bailegangaire and how it came by its appellation

Bailegangaire was first performed by Druid in Galway on the 5th of December 1985 with the following cast:

Mommo	Siobhán McKenna
Mary	Marie Mullen
Dolly	Mary McEvoy

Directed by	Garry Hynes
Designed by	Frank Conway
Lighting by	Roger Frith

Subsequent major productions of this play have been:

1999	Royal Court Theatre, London, directed by James McDonald
2001	Abbey Theatre, Dublin, directed by Tom Murphy – part of 'Tom Murphy at the Abbey'
2002	The Irish Repertory Theatre, New York, directed by Tom Murphy

Bailegangaire was revived by Druid in Galway on the 11th of September 2014, with the following cast:

Mommo	Marie Mullen
Mary	Catherine Walsh
Dolly	Aisling O'Sullivan

Directed by	Garry Hynes
Set & Costume by	Francis O'Connor
Lighting by	Rick Fisher
Sound by	Gregory Clarke

Characters

Mommo
Mary
Dolly

Time and place: 1984, the kitchen of a thatched house. The set should be stylised to avoid cliché and to achieve best effect.

Note: 'Notturno' in E Flat by Schubert introduces and closes the play. Mary's poem, which she misquotes, in Act One is 'Silences' by Thomas Hardy.

Act One

Dusk is setting in on a room, a country kitchen. There are some modern conveniences: a cooker, a radio (which is switched on), electric light – a single pendant. Photographs on the walls, brown photographs. There is a double bed. It is the warmest room in the house (probably the central room of the traditional three-roomed thatched house). An old woman in the bed, **Mommo**, *is eating and drinking something out of a mug, occasionally rejecting pieces of food, spitting them on the floor. She is a good mimic.*

Mommo   *Shkoth caoc*! *Shkoth*! (*Driving imagined hens from the house.*) Dirty aul' things about the place . . . And for all they lay!

She is senile.

Mary, *her granddaughter, wears a wrap-around apron draped tightly about her spinster frame; bare knees over half Wellington boots; hair tight, perhaps in a bun. She is forty-one. A 'private' person, an intelligent, sensitive woman, a trier, but one who is near breaking point.*

Mommo *has interrupted her meal, this time to talk to imagined children at the foot of the bed.*

Mommo   Let ye be settling now, my fondlings, and I'll be giving ye a nice story again tonight when I finish this. An' ye'll be goin' to sleep.

The kettle is boiling. **Mary** *makes tea, lays the table. She produces the anomaly of a silver teapot.* **Mommo** *is now watching* **Mary** *and* **Mary**'s *movements suspiciously.*

Mommo   . . . An' no one will stop me! Tellin' my nice story . . . (*Reverts to herself.*) Yis, how the place called Bochtán – and its *graund* ('grand') inhabitants – came to its new appellation, Bailegangaire, the place without laughter. Now! . . . Jolter-headed gobshites . . . What time is it?

Mary   Seven.

Mary is *taking off her apron.*

Mommo   Yis! *Shkoth*! an' lock them in. Hah-haa! but I'll outdo the fox, I'll take the head of the everyone of them hens tomorrow.

Mary   Mommo? (*She has removed her apron and in her new image is smiling bravely against an increasing sense of loneliness and demoralisation.*) I have a surprise for you.

Mommo   Pardon?

Mary   Look! (*She holds up an iced cake.*) We never knew your birthday but today is mine and I thought we might share the same birthday together in future. (*She has lit a candle.*)

Mommo (*eyes fixed on the candle*)   The cursèd paraffin.

Mary   Though someone once said – I may be wrong – yours was the first of May, a May child.

Mommo   The cursèd paraffin.

Mary   And you can get up for a while – if you wish.

Mommo   Birthday?

Mary   Yes! We'll have a party, the two of us.

Mommo   What's birthdays to do with us?

Mary   By candlelight.

Mommo   What's your business here?

Mary (*indicating the table*)   Isn't that nice?

Mommo   Do I know you?

Mary   Mary. (*She bows her head momentarily deflated, then smiles invitingly at* **Mommo** *again.*) Hmm?

Mommo (*and there is defiance, hatred in the sound*). Heh heh heh heh!

Mary   Mary. (*Deflated. And sits.*)

We get the end of the news in Irish on the radio, then Tommy O'Brien's programme of light classics, Your Choice and Mine. *The candlelight, the table neatly laid, the silver teapot, the simple line of* **Mary***'s dress becomes her, a book beside her, sipping tea, the grave intelligent face, a picture of strange, elegant loneliness.*

Mommo   Ooh! and to be sure and so as not to be putting any over-enlargement on my narrative, the creatures left in that place now can still *smile,* on occasion. And to be sure, the childre, as is the wont of all childre in God's kingdom on earth, are as clever at the laughing as they are at the crying, until they arrive at the age of reason. That is well, my dears. Here! You! Miss! Take this. Did you manage to poison me? Ha-haa – No – Ho-ho!

Mary *takes a cup of tea to* **Mommo** *and places it on the chair beside the bed, takes the mug and returns to the table. A car passes by outside.*

Mommo (*settles herself in the bed for her story*)   Now to tell my story! (*In storyteller's mode:*) It was a bad year for the crops, a good one for mushrooms and the contrary and adverse connection between these two is always the case. So you can be sure the people were putting their store in the poultry and the *bonavs* ('bonhams') and the creamery produce for the great *maragadh mór* ('big market') that is held every year on the last Saturday before Christmas in *Bailethuama* ('the town of Tuam') in the other county. And some sold well and some sold middlin', and one couple was in it – strangers, ye understand – sold not at all. And at day's business concluded there was celebration, for some, and fitting felicitations exchanged, though not of the usual protraction, for all had an eye on the cold inclement weather that boded. So, the people were departing Bailethuama in the other county in diverse directions homewards. As were the people of the place I'm talking about. And they were only middlin' satisfied, if at all. The Bocháns were never entirely fortunate. An' devil mend them. An' scald them. No matter. What time is it? . . . Miss!

Mary   Seven – (*The tips of her fingers to her forehead.*) – Eight.

Mommo   Supa tea.

Mary   It's on the chair beside you.

Mommo   I'm waiting for someone. Oh an' he *will* come yet. (*A warning to* **Mary**.) And he has a big stick.

Mary (*remains seated: she knows from experience what the outcome of the conversation is going to be; she does not lift her eyes*)   And time to take your pills.

Mommo (*has no intention of taking them*)   The yellow ones?

Mary   Yes.

Mommo   They're good for me?

Mary   I'll give you a cigarette.

Mommo   They'll help me sleep?

Mary   Yes.

Mommo   Heh heh heh heh!

Mary (*to herself*)   And I'd like to read, Mommo.

Mommo (*in storyteller's mode*)   Now there was a decent man at that market and his decent wife the same. Strangers, strangers! Sure they could have come from the south of – Galway! – for all I know. And they had sold not at all. Well, if you call the one basket of pullets' eggs valiant trade. (*She takes a sip of the tea.*) Too hot. No. Their main cargo which consisted of eighteen snow-white geese still lay trussed in the floor of the cart, *gus bhár ar an mí-ádh sin* ('and to make matters worse') the pitch on an incline of the road was proving an impossibility for the horse to surmount. But he was a decent man, and he took not belt – nor the buckle-end of it as another would – to the noble animal that is the horse. Put it down! (*The last to* **Mary** *who is standing by having put a little more milk into* **Mommo**'s *tea.*) No. But spoke only in the gentlest of terms, encouraging the poor beast to try once more against the adversary. 'Try again, Pedlar.' For that was the horse's name. (*In a conversational mode:*) Is that a step?

Mary (*listening*)   Dolly was to call last night. (*The sound they have heard – if any – does not materialise further.*) Nobody. She didn't call the night before either.

Mommo   What's this?

Mary *does not understand.*

Mommo   Taking down the good cup!

Mary   It tastes nicer out of a –

Mommo   Mug, a mug! – oh leave it so now! Put it down!

Mary   And nicer to have your pills with.

Mommo   The yellow ones – try again, Pedlar, for-that-was-the-horse's name!

Mary *returns to the table.*

Mommo (*in storyteller's mode*)   And all the while his decent wife on the grass verge and she *cráite* ('crestfallen'). And a detail which you may contemplate fondly now but was only further testimonial to the misfortunes of that unhappy couple, each time she went to draw the shawl more tightly round her frailty, the hand peepin' out held three sticks of rock. Now! Yis, gifts for her care, three small waiting grandchildren. Like ye. Isn't it a good one? (*A sip of tea.*) Cold.

Mary (*to herself*)   I can't stand it.

But she is up again to add a little hot water to the tea.

Mommo   And she up to the fifty mark!

Mary (*to herself*)   And that bitch Dolly.

Mommo (*reflectively*)   Or was she maybe more?

Mary   In heat again.

Mommo   And what was her husband? Decorous efficiency in all he cared to turn his hand to, like all small men. Sure he had topped the sixty!

Mary   Taste that and see if it's alright for you.

Mommo   But he was unlucky. He was. He was. An' times, maybe, she was unkind to him. (*Childlike.*) Was she?

Mary   No. (*Returning to the table where she sits, her head back on her shoulders, looking up at the ceiling.*)

Mommo   And how many children had she bore herself?

Mary   Eight?

Mommo   And what happened to them?

Mary   Nine? Ten?

Mommo   Hah?

Mary   What happened us all?

Mommo   Them (that) weren't drowned or died they said she drove away.

Mary   Mommo?

Mommo   Let them say what they like.

Mary   I'm Mary. I'm very happy here.

Mommo   Oh but she looked after her grandchildren. Tom is in Galway. He's afeared of the gander.

Mary   Mommo? Please stop. Because I'm so lonely.

Mommo   To *continue*. (*In storyteller's mode:*) Now man and horse, though God knows they tried, could see the icy hill was not for yielding. So what was there for doing but to retrace the hard-won steps to the butt-end of the road which, as matters would have it, was a fork. One road leading up the incline whence they came, the other to Bochtán. Now that man knew that the road to Bochtán, though of circularity, was another means home. And it looked level enough stretching out into the gathering duskess. And 'deed he knew men from his own village (who) had travelled it and got home safe and sound. Still he

paused. Oh not through fear, for if he was a man to submit
he would've threwn himself into the river years ago. No. But
in gentleness, sad the searching eye on the road. And sadder
still the same grey eyes were growing in handsomeness as
the years went by. She had noted it. But she'd never
comment on this becoming aspect of his mien for, strange, it
saddened her too. It did. But the two little smiles appearing,
one each side of his mouth, before taking a step anywhere.
Even when only to go to the back door last thing at night an'
call in the old dog to the hearth.

Mary *hears the 'putt-putt' of a motorcycle approaching, stopping
outside.*

Mary   Right!

Suggesting she is going to have matters out with **Dolly**. *She puts on
her apron, gets bucket, water, scrubbing brush, to scrub the part of
the floor that* **Mommo** *spat on.*

Mommo   An' then the silence, save the tick of the clock . . .
(*Reflectively.*) An' why didn't she break it? She knew how to
use the weapon of silence. But why didn't he? A woman isn't
stick or stone. The gap in the bed, concern for the morrow,
how to keep the one foot in front of the other. An' when
would it all stop. What was the dog's name? (*Childlike.*) D'ye
know I can't remember.

Dolly   Mo Dhuine.

Dolly *has come in. Like her name, she is dolled up in gaudy, rural
fashion. She is thirty-nine. She has a handbag and she carries a
crash helmet.*

Mommo   Shep, was it?

Dolly   Mo Dhuine.

Mommo   Spot? Rover? Mo Dhuine! Mo Dhuine! Now!
Mo Dhuine.

Dolly   Jesus! (*To herself.*)

Mommo   He loved Mo Dhuine – Hona ho gus ha-haa! (*Laughing in celebration.*) An' the bother an' the care on him one time filling the eggshell with the hot ember an' leavin' it there by the door.

Dolly   Then the root in the arse –

Mommo   Then the root in the arse to poor Mo Dhuine, the twig 'cross his back, to get along with him an' the mouth burned in him! Oh but it did, *did,* cured him of thievin' the eggs.

Dolly *switches on the light.* **Mommo**'s *eyes to the light bulb.*

Dolly   What're yeh doin' workin' in the dark?

Mommo (*in storyteller's mode*)   But they had to get home.

Dolly   Oh, she can't have everything her own way.

Mommo   Their inheritance, the three small waiting children, left unattended.

Dolly (*rooting in her bag, producing a bottle of vodka*)   How yeh!

Mary *merely nods, continues working.*

Mommo   And night fast closing around them.

Dolly   Stronger she's gettin'. A present.

Mary (*hopeful that the vodka is for her birthday*)   For what?

Dolly   'Cause I couldn't come up last night.

Mary   What do I! (want with a bottle of vodka)

Dolly   Yeh never know. She'll last for ever.

Mommo   Then, drawing a deep breath. (*She draws a deep breath.*) Oh but didn't give vent to it, for like the man he was I'm sayin', refusing to *sigh* or submit. An', 'On we go, Pedlar' says he, an' man, horse, cart and the woman falling in 'tween the two hind shafts set off on the road to Bochtán which place did not come by its present appellation, Bailegangaire, till that very night. Now.

Dolly   Jesus, Bailegangaire – D'yeh want a fag? – night after night, can't you stop her? A fag?

Mary (*declines the cigarette*)   No.

Dolly   Night after night the same old story – (*Proffering cigarettes again.*) Ary you might as well.

Mary *ignores her.*

Dolly   By Jesus I'd stop her.

Mary   I wish you'd stop using that word, Dolly. I've been trying to stop her. (*Putting away bucket, etc.*)

Dolly   Michaeleen is sick. The tonsils again. So I couldn't come up last night. I'm worried about them tonsils. What d'yeh think? So I can't stay long tonight either.

Mary   Aren't you going to say hello to her?

Dolly   What's up with yeh? *Home,* I'm goin'.

Mary   Aren't you going to take off your coat?

Dolly   What do you mean?

Mary   What do you mean what do I mean!

Dolly *turns stubbornly into the fire and sits.*

Mommo   But to come to Bochtán so ye'll have it all. Them from that place had been to the market were 'riving back home. One of them, a Séamus Costello by name. Oh, a fine strappin' man. Wherever he got it from. The size an' the breadth of him, you'd near have to step into the verge to give him sufficient right-of-way. 'Twould be no use him extending the civility 'cause you'd hardly get around him I'm saying. And he was liked. Rabbits he was interested in. This to his widowed mother's dismay, but that's another thing. And the kind of man that when people'd espy him approaching the gurgle'd be already startin' in their mouths – 'Och-haw'. For he was the exception, ye understand, with humour in him as big as himself. And I'm thinkin' he was the one an' only boast they ever had in that cursèd place. (*In a conversational mode:*) What time is it?

Mary } Eight!

Dolly } Nine!

They look at each other, laugh, and bygones are bygones.

Mary   Quarter past eight.

Mommo   Quarter past eight, an' sure that's not late. That's a rhyme. Now for ye! (*She takes a sip of tea.*) Too sweet.

Mary *rectifying the tea situation. A cajoling tone coming into* **Dolly**'s *voice – there's something on her mind, and she is watching and assessing* **Mary** *privately.*

Dolly   They say it's easier to do it for someone else's (*to take care of a stranger*). And that old story is only upsetting her, Mary, isn't it? (*Declining tea which* **Mary** *offers.*) No thanks.

Mary *is too intelligent to be taken in by* **Dolly**'s *tone or tactics – but this is not at issue here: she has other things on her mind. She sits by the fire with* **Dolly** *and now accepts the cigarette.* **Mommo** *is sipping tea.*

Dolly   Harping on misery, and only wearing herself out. And you. Amn't I right, Mary? And she never finishes it – Why doesn't she finish it and have done with it? For God's sake!

Mary *considers this ('Finish it and have done with it?'), then forgets it for the moment. She is just looking into the fire.*

Mary   I'd love to have a talk.

Dolly   About what?

Mary   Do you remember . . . (*She shakes her head: she does not know.*)

Dolly   What? . . . I know it affects you: Like, her not reco'nisin' you ever – Why wouldn't it? But you were away a long time.

Mary *looks up: she has been only half listening.*

Dolly   That's the reason.

Mary   . . . I've often thought . . . (*She is just looking at the fire again.*)

Dolly   What?

Mary   I may have been too – bossy – at first.

Dolly   Well, well, there could be something in that, too.

Mary   But I wanted to . . . bring about change. Comfort, civilised.

Dolly   Yes, well, but. Though I don't know. You were away an awful long time. I was left holdin' the can. Like, when yeh think of it, you owe me a very big debt.

Mary (*looks up*)   Hmm? A very big?

Dolly   I mean that's why she reco'nises me.

Mary *looking at the fire again;* **Dolly** *watching* **Mary**. *Something on* **Dolly**'s *mind; she coughs in preparation to speak –*

Mary   We had a pony and trap once. The Sunday outings. You don't remember?

Dolly, *puzzled, shakes her head.*

Mary   Ribbons. Grandad would always bring ribbons home for our hair. You don't remember.

Dolly   . . . You work too hard.

Mary *laughs at* **Dolly**'s *explanation of it all.*

Dolly   What? (*Laughing because* **Mary** *has laughed.*)

Mary *shakes her head, 'it doesn't matter'.*

Dolly   And you're too serious.

Mary   Do you remember Daddy?

Dolly   Well, the photographs. (*They look about at the photographs on the wall.*) Aul' brown ghosts. (*Playful, but cajoling.*) Y'are, y'are, too serious.

Mary (*eyes back to the fire*)   I suppose I am. I don't know what I'm trying to say. (*Sighs.*) Home!

Mommo (*puts down her cup*)   And that, too, is well. (*In storyteller's mode:*) And now with his old jiggler of a bicycle set again' the gable, Costello was goin' in to John Mah'ny's, the one and only shop for everything for miles around. 'Cold enough for ye, ladies!' Now! Cold enough for ye, ladies. And that was the first remark he was to utter that evening. And the two women he had thus accosted set to gurgling at once and together. 'Caw och-caw, Seamusheen a wockeen, God bless yeh, och-caw,' says the old crone that was in it buyin' the salt. And, 'Uck-uck-uck, uck-uck hunuka huckina-caw, Costello' from the young buxom woman tendin' the shop end of the counter, and she turnin' one of the babes in her arms so that he too could behold the hero. 'Aren't they gettin' awful big, God bless them,' then saying Costello of the two twins an' they gogglin' at him. 'Jack Frost is coming with a vengeance for ye tonight,' says he, 'or the Bogey Man maybe bejingoes.' And to the four or five others now holding tight their mother's apron, 'Well, someone is comin' anyways,' says he, 'if ye all aren't good.' An' then off with him to the end where the drink was.

Dolly   Good man, Josie!

Mary   No!

Mommo   } 'Good man, Josie!'

Mary   Don't encourage her.

Mommo   } NOW!

Mary   I'm! (*going out of my mind*).

Mommo   } Good man, Josie.

Mary   I'm trying to stop it!

Mommo   } And that was the second greeting he uttered that night.

Mary   } Talk to her!

Dolly   That's what I try to do!

Mommo   He got no reply.

Dolly (*going to* **Mommo**, *under her breath*)   Good man, Josie, Jesus!

Mommo   Nor did he expect one.

Dolly (*calling back to* **Mary**)   And I'm going at quarter to nine! – Good man, Mommo, how's it cuttin'?

Mommo   Good man – ! Pardon?

Dolly   How's the adversary treatin' yeh?

Mommo (*to herself*)   Good man, Mommo?

Dolly   I brought yeh sweets.

Mommo   There's nothing wrong with me.

Dolly   I didn't say there was.

Mommo   An' I never done nothin' wrong.

Dolly   Sweets!

Mary   Butterscotch, isn't it, Dolly?

Mommo (*to herself, puzzled again*)   Good man – *Who?*

Dolly   Butterscotch, I've oceans of money.

Mary   Your favourites.

Dolly   You like them ones.

Mary   Try one. You (**Dolly**) give it to her.

Mommo   Do I like them ones?

Mary   Suck it slowly.

Dolly   Gob-stoppers I should have brought her.

Mary   Shh!

Dolly   You're lookin' fantastic. (*Going back to the fire.*) It'd be a blessing if she went.

Mary (*placatory*)   Shh, don't say things like (that). Talk to her, come on.

Dolly   About what? It's like an oven in here – and I don't understand a word she's sayin'.

Mary   Take off your – (coat).

Dolly   I – don't – want – to – take – off – my!

Mary   Tell her about the children.

Dolly   *Seafóid*, nonsense talk about forty years ago –

Mary   Come on –

Dolly   And I've enough problems of my own. Why don't you stick her in there? (*One of the other rooms.*)

Mary   It's damp. And she understands – recognises you a lot of the time.

Dolly *rolling her eyes but following* **Mary** *back to the bed again.*

Mary   Where she can see you.

Dolly   Well, the children are all fine, Mommo. (*A slip.*) Well, Michaeleen is sick, the tonsils again. I've rubberbacked lino in all the bedrooms now, the Honda is going like a bomb and the *lounge,* my dear, is carpeted. I seen the lean and lanky May Glynn, who never comes near ye or this house, in her garden when I was motoring over but she went in without a salute. I must have distemper too or whatever. Conor, that other lean and lanky bastard, is now snaking his fence in another six inches, and my darlin' mother-in-law, old sharp-eyes-and-the-family rosary, sends her pers'nal blessings to ye both.

Mary   Is she babysitting for you?

Dolly   No. She is not babysitting for me. (I don't want her or any of the McGrath clan in my house.)

Mommo (*sucking the sweet*)   They're nice.

Dolly   An' the cat had kittens. (*To* **Mary**.) D'yeh want a kitten? Do you, Mommo? (*A touch of sour introversion.*) Does anyone? Before I drown them.

Mommo   Tom is in Galway.

Mary   Did you hear from Stephen?

Dolly   The 'wire' again on Friday, regular as clockwork.

Mary   Did you hear, Mommo?

Mommo   I did. But she told May Glynn not to be waitin', her own mother'd be needin' her, and that they'd be home before dark for sure.

Dolly   Hundred-and-thirty-five quid a week and never a line.

Mary   He's busy.

Dolly   Fuck him. I don't know what to do with the money! (*Sour introspection again.*) Or do I? I've started saving for a purpose. (*Then impetuously to* **Mary**.) Do *you* want some money? Well, do you, Mommo? To go dancin'.

Mary *is laughing at her sister's personality.*

Mary   Stephen will be home as usual for Christmas.

Dolly   For his goose.

Mary   Won't he, Mommo?

Mommo (*to herself*)   Stephen, yes, fugum.

They laugh. Then, **Dolly***, grimly:*

Dolly   Well maybe it'd be better if the bold Stephen skipped his visit home this Christmas. (*Rises and turns her back on them.*) Jesus, misfortunes.

Mary *now wondering, her eyes on* **Dolly**'s *back, the stout figure.*

Mommo (*to herself*)   Yes. Misfortunes.

Mary   Dolly?

Dolly   Ooh, a cake, a candle – candles! what's the occasion? (*She gives a kiss to* **Mommo**.) Well, I'm off now, darlin', an' God an' all his holy saints protect an' bless yeh.

Mommo (*buried in her own thoughts until now*)   When did you arrive?

Dolly   What?

Mommo   When did you arrive?

Dolly   I arrived –

Mommo   Sure you're welcome, when did you arrive?

Dolly   I arrived –

Mommo   Well did yeh?

Dolly   I did.

Mommo   From where?

Dolly   From –

Mommo   Now. And is that where y'are now?

Dolly   The very location.

Mommo   Now! I never knew that. Where?

Dolly   Ahm . . . Aw Jesus, Mommo, you have us all as confused as yourself! Ballindine! Ball-in-dine.

Mommo   Hah? Oh yes, yeh told me. Now. Who are you?

Dolly   Dolly, I think.

Mommo (*considering this, sucking her sweet*)   Now. Dolly.

Dolly   Dolly!

Mommo   Yes.

Dolly   Look, I have to be – (going) I'm Dolly, your granddaughter, and that's Mary, your other granddaughter, and your grandson Tom, Tom is dead.

Mary   Shh!

Dolly   Ah, shh! (*To* **Mommo**.) Now do you know?

Mommo   I do. I'm waiting for someone.

Dolly   Who're yeh waiting for?

Mommo   I'm not tellin' yeh.

Dolly   A man, is it?

Mommo (*laughing*)   'Tis.

Dolly   Ahona ho gus hah-haa, an' what'll he have for yeh!

Mommo (*laughing*)   A big stick.

Dolly   M-m-m-m! – A big stick, the bata! Mmmah! (*Sexual innuendo*.) Now! Try that subject on her if you want to stop her.

Mommo   Oh but they were always after me.

Dolly   An' did they ketch yeh?

Mommo   The ones I wanted to.

Dolly   An' are they still after yeh?

Mommo   But I bolt the door – on some of them. (*Laughing*.)

Dolly (*to* **Mary**)   That's what all the aul ones like to talk about. I think you're goin' soft in the head.

Mommo (*recognising her*)   Is it Dolly? Aw is it my Dolly! Well, d'yeh know I didn't rec'nise yeh. Sure you were always the joker. Aw, my Dolly, Dolly, Dolly, come 'ere to me!

Dolly *hesitates, is reluctant, then succumbs to the embrace; indeed, after a moment she is clinging tightly to the old woman.* **Mary** *stands by, isolated, watching the scene. She would love to be included. The smallest gesture of affection or recognition would help greatly.*

Mommo   Ah, lovee. Lovee, lovee, lovee. Sure if I knew you were comin' – (*Aside to* **Mary**.) Will you put on the kettle, will you? Standing there! – I'd've baked a cake. That's an old one. Oh, mo pheata (*my pet*). Why didn't you send word? An' you got fat. You did! On me oath! Will you put on the kettle, Miss, will you! (*Whispering*.) Who is that woman?

Dolly (*tearfully, but trying to joke*)   She's the sly one.

Mommo   She is. (*Loudly, hypocritically*.) Isn't she nice?

Dolly   Watch her.

Mary *goes off to another room.*

Mommo   Why is she interfering?

Dolly   Shh, Mommo.

Mommo   Be careful of that one.

Dolly   Shh, Mommo, I'm in terrible trouble.

Mommo   Yes, watch her.

Dolly (*extricating herself from the embrace, brushing away a tear*)   Leave her to me. I'll deal with her. (*Calls*.) Miss! Will you come out, will you, an' make a brew! An' put something in it! Sure you should know about all kinds of potions.

Mary *has returned with a suitcase. She places it somewhere.*

Dolly   . . . Someone going on a *voyage*?

Mary   I have to come to a decision, Dolly.

Dolly   Again?

Mary   She's your responsibility too.

Dolly   I know you think I inveigled you back here so that Stephen and I could escape.

Mary   No one inveigled me anywhere. You're not pulling your weight.

Dolly (*shrugs*)   There's always the County Home.

Mary   You –

Dolly   Wouldn't I? Why should I stick myself again back in here?

Mary   Why should I?

Dolly   In a place like this.

Mary   Why do I? In a place like this.

Dolly (*shrugs*)   That's your business. Well, I have to be going.

Mary   I'd like to go out sometimes too.

Dolly   *Home,* I'm going.

Mary   You look it.

Dolly   Alright, I'll tell you, so that you can go, where the man is waiting.

Mary   Man? *Men!*

Dolly *shrugs, is moving off.*

Mary   I need to talk to – *someone!*

Dolly (*her back to* **Mary**; *quietly*)   I need to talk to someone too.

Mary (*an insinuation*)   Why don't you take off your coat?

Dolly (*faces* **Mary**; *a single solemn nod of her head; then*)   Because, now, I am about to leave. I'll figure out something. I might even call back in a while, 'cause it doesn't take long, does it? Just a few minutes; that's all it takes.

Mary   You're disgusting.

Dolly   Am I?

Mary (*going to one of the other rooms*)   I've *come* to a decision. (*Off.*) County Home! You won't blackmail me!

Dolly (*to herself*)   I hate this house. (*To* **Mommo**.) Good man, Josie!

Mommo   Oh yes. 'Good man, Josie!'

Dolly (*going out; an undertone*)   Ah, fuck it all.

Mommo   Now! (*Storytelling mode:*) Good man, Josie. And that was the second greeting Costello was to utter that evening.

Mary (*coming in*)   I'll leave everything here for you spick and span, of course.

She has not heard **Dolly** *go out; now she stands there looking at the door, the motorcycle outside driving away, her hands clapping together some of her wardrobe (as if demonstrating the possibility that she is leaving rather than confirming it).*

Mommo   He got no reply. Nor did he expect one. For Josie was a Greaney and none was ever right in that fambly.

Mary   It's not fair. (*To herself.*)

Mommo   An' the threadbare fashion'ry, not a top-coat to him, the shirt neck open.

Mary (*to herself*)   Not a gansey.

Mommo   Nor a gansey.

Mary   *Nor* a gansey.

Mommo   An' the tuthree raggedy topcoats on the others. Though some say he had the knack of mendin' clocks – if he had.

Mary (*angrily: still to the door*)   Your husband wined, dined and bedded me! Stephen? *Your* Stephen?! It was *me* he wanted! But I told him: 'Keep off! Stop following me!' That's why he took you!

Mommo (*she has had a sip of tea*)   What's in this? Miss!

Mary   The County Home! (*Gesturing, meaning did* **Mommo** *hear what* **Dolly** *said.*)

Mommo   Hot drink, decent supa tea!

Mary (*automatically sets about making fresh tea, then she stops*)   I have *come* to a decision I said! Do you understand? So if you could wait a moment. (*She starts to discard some of the clothes, packing others; talking to herself again.*) Just to see who is in earnest this time. And I was doing well – I was the success! Now I'm talking to myself.

Mommo (*storytelling mode:*)   Howandever. 'How the boys!' was Costello's third greeting. This time to two old men with their heads in the fire. The one of them givin' out the odd aul' sigh, smoking his pipe with assiduity and beating the slow obsequies of a death-roll with his boot. An' the other, a Brian by name, replying in sagacity, 'Oh yis,' sharing the silent mysteries of the world between them. (*In conversational mode:*) Me mouth is (dry), d'ye know.

Mary   Just a moment! (*Going to other room.*) Dependent on a pension and that bitch.

Mommo   Where is she? Miss!

Mary (*off*)   Miss! Miss! Miss is coming! (*Entering with more clothes.*) Miss: as if I didn't exist. That's the thanks I get, that's the – (*Winces to herself.*) It's – not – thanks I'm looking for. (*Absently.*) What am I looking for? I had to come home. No one inveigled me. I wanted to come home.

Exasperated, she comes out of her reverie, dumps her clothes and sets about making more tea.

And you know very well who I am! You do! You do!

Mommo   Sure it's often I'd be watchin' me own father engaged in the same practice, drawing wisdom from the fire. 'Deed, on one such occasion, an 'twas maybe a full hour's contemplation, he craned his neck, the glaze to his eyes, to accost me with the philosophy that was troublin' him. 'How much does a seagull weigh?' I held my silence to be sure, for times he'd get cross – oh he'd welt yeh with the stick – if a guess was attempted or a sound itself uttered. For he wouldn't be talkin' to you at all. The groans out of that man decipherin' the enigmal. Then, at last, when he found for himself the answer to the riddle he declared in 'sured solemnity, 'I'm thinkin' two ounces.' Now! That's who I'm waiting for. Oh, men have their ways and women their places an' that is God's plan, my bright ones.

She has got out of bed. **Mary** *sees her and is hurrying to her assistance.*

Mommo   Shhtaap!

Mary *is stopped by the ferocity.* **Mommo** *squats, hidden behind the headboard of the bed (perhaps on a commode).*

Mary   . . . And to change your nightdress . . . I was a nurse, Mommo . . . And offers of marriage.

Then, quickly, efficiently, she takes the opportunity of remaking the bed. She replaces the sheets with clean ones, removes the bed-warmer – which is a cast-iron lid of a pot in a knitted woollen cover; she puts the lid into the fire to reheat it. She appears almost happy when she is working constructively, and she starts to recite:

'There is the silence of copse or croft
When the wind sinks dumb.
And of belfry loft
When the tenor after tolling stops its hum.
And there's the silence of a lonely pond
Where a man was drowned . . .'

And sure you have lots of poems, lots of stories, nice stories, instead of that old one. 'Mick Delaney' – Do you remember that one? We loved that one. How did it begin? Or ghost stories. People used to come *miles* to hear you tell stories. Oh! And do you remember: the gramophone? Yes, we had a gramophone too. 'The banshee is out tonight go down (*on*) your knees and say your prayers – Wooooo!' Or would you like me to read you a story?

Mommo (*reappearing from behind the bed*)   Heh heh heh heh!

Mary   Why can't you be civil to me? At least tonight. There was happiness here too, Mommo. Harmony?

Mommo (*straight back, neck craned*)   You can be going now, Miss.

Mary   . . . Alright.

She collects the chamber pot from behind the headboard of the bed and goes out.

Mommo   She knows too much about our business entirely. (*She calls hypocritically.*) And thank you! (*Giggles getting back into the bed.*) Now amn't I able for them? (*Storytelling mode:*) But now that Costello was in it the aspect was transforming. 'An',' says old Brian, taking his head out of the fire, 'what's the news from the Big World?' 'The Dutch has taken Holland!' says Costello with such a rumble out of him near had the whole house shook asunder and all in it in ululation so infectious was the sound. Save Josie who was heedless, but rapping with severity on the counter for more libation. And 'John!' says the young buxom woman, calling to her husband – 'John!' – to come out and tend his end of the counter, an' she now putting questions on bold Costello. 'You wor in Tuam?' says she, 'I was in Tuam,' says he, 'Yeh wor?' says she, 'I was,' says he, 'An' how was it?' says she. 'Well, not tellin' you a word of a lie now,' says he, 'but 'twas deadly.' And 'Ory!' says the crone that was in it buyin' the salt. 'Did yeh hear?' says the young buxom woman to her husband, John, to be sure. He had 'rived from the kitchen an' was frownin' pullin' pints. Merchants d'ye know: good market or bad, the arithmetic in the ledger has to come out correct. 'Well do yeh tell me so?' says the young buxom woman. 'I do tell yeh so,' says Costello. 'Talkin' about a Maragadh Mór? – I never in all me born days seen light or likes of it!' Now they were listening.

Mary *comes in. She selects her 'going-away' suit. She tries the waist against herself. She puts the suit on a chair beside the fire to air it. Through the following she goes out/comes in with turf for the night.*

Mommo   'Firkins of butter,' says he, 'an' cheese be the hundred-weight. Ducks, geese, chickens, *bonavs* and – Geese!' says he, 'geese! There was hundreds of them! There was hundreds upon hundreds of thousands of them! The ground I tell ye was white with them!' And 'White with them,' says the crone. 'They went ch-cheap then?' says John, still bowed frownin' over the tricks of pullin' porter. 'Cheap then?' says Costello, 'sure yeh couldn't give them away sure. Sure the sight of so many chickens an' geese an'! Sure all the people could do was stand and stare.' 'They were puzzled,' says the crone. 'I'm tellin' ye,' says Costello, 'Napoleon Bonaparte wouldn't have said no to all the provisions goin' a-beggin' in that town of Tuam today.' An' 'Hah?' says John, squintin', the head-work interrupted. 'On his retreat from Moscow, sure,' says Costello. 'Or Josephine – Wuw! – neither.' Now! Wuw. Them were his ways, an' he having the others equivalently pursuant: 'Wo ho ho, wo ho ho!' 'But you sis-sold your rabbits, did yeh, Costello?' says John. An' wasn't there a gap. Oh, only for the second. 'Oh I sold them,' then sayin' Costello. 'Oh I did, did,' saying he, 'Oh on me solemn 'n dyin' oath! Every man-jack-rabbit of them.' Like a man not to be believed, his bona fides in question. 'Yeh-yeh codjer yeh-yeh,' says John. Whatever he meant. But he was not at all yet feeling cordial. But thus was the night faring into its progression, others 'riving back home an' how did they do an' who else was in it, did they buy e'er a thing, Costello settin' them laughin', John frownin' an' squintin', an' the thief of a Christmas they wor all goin' t'have. (*Conversational mode:*) What're ye doin' there?

Mary *is putting the dirty bed linen into a bucket to soak. She holds up a sheet and bucket to show* **Mommo**.

Mommo   Hah? . . . There's nothing here for people to be prying in corners for. Bring in the brishen of turf for the night an' then you may go home to your own house.

Mary   Alright.

She moves as if going out the door, then silently to the comparative dark of the far corner where she remains motionless.

Mommo   You couldn't be up to them. (*She yawns:*) Oh ho huneo! (*Storytelling mode:*) An' twas round about now the rattlin' of the horse an' cart was heard abroad on the road an' had them in the shop peepin' at the windy. 'Twas the decent man an' his decent wife the same was in it. And 'Stand, Pedlar,' says the man in (a) class of awesome whisper. And his decent wife from the heel of the cart to his side to view the spectre was now before them. The aspect silver of moon an' stars reflecting off the new impossibility. Loughran's Hill. Creature. She now clutching more tightly the sweets to her breast. (*She yawns again; her eyes close.*)

Mary (*whispers*)   Sleep.

Mommo (*eyes open*)   Hah? *Now* what was there for doing? Which way to cast the hopeful eye? No-no, not yet, in deliberate caution, would he acknowledge the shop, John Mah'ny's, forninst them, but looked behind him the road they came, forward again, but to what avail? There was only John Mah'ny's now for his contemplation, nature all around them serenely waiting, and didn't the two little smiles come appearing again.

Mary (*whispers*)   Sleep.

Mommo   Hah?

Mary   Sleep, sleep, peace, peace.

Mommo   An' the strangers, that decent man an' his decent wife the same, rounded the gable into the merchant's yard, an' sorry the night that was the decision. What time is it? . . . She's gone. An' she can stay gone. But them are the details, c'rrect to the particular. And they can be vouched for. For there was to be many's the inquisition by c'roner, civic guard and civilian on all that transpired in John Mah'ny's that night. Now. (*She yawns:*) Wasn't that a nice story? An' we'll all be goin' to sleep.

She is asleep

Mary (*looking at* **Mommo**)   Sleep? For how long? . . . (*Testing* **Mommo**:) 'Now as all do know the world over'?

Mary *switches off the radio. She switches off the light. She goes to the table and idly starts lighting candles on the cake, using a new match to light each one. A car passes by outside. She blows out the candles, tires of them. Now what to do? . . .*

Mary (*Idly at first:*)   Now as all do know the world over . . . Now as all do know . . . Now as all do know the world over the custom when entering the house of another is to invoke our Maker's benediction on all present. (*Adds a piece of sardonic humour:*) Save the cat. Well, as the Bochtáns would have it later, no mention of our Maker, or His Blessed Son, was mentioned by the strangers as they came 'cross John Mahoney's *threshel* ('threshold') that night. But no, no, no, no, no. No now! They were wrongin' that couple. (*To the sleeping* **Mommo**.) Weren't they? They were. They wor. (*To* **Mommo**.) And when you. And when that decent woman gave the whole story to her father, what did he say? (*A touch of mimicry of* **Mommo**.) An' believe *you* me he knew all about them. That them Bochtáns were a venomous pack of jolter-headed gobshites. Didn't he? He did. An ill-bred band of amadans an' oinseachs – untutored in science, philosophy or the fundamental rudimentaries of elementary husbandry itself. A low crew of illiterate plebs, drunkards and incestuous bastards, and would ever continue as such, improper and despicable in their incorrigibility. They're not nice, he said. Supa tea. (*She pours a glass of vodka for herself.*) And he was the man to give the tongue-lashin'. An' 'twas from him I got my learnin'. That's who I'm waitin' for. (*She has a sip of the vodka.*) Too sweet. (*She dilutes the vodka with water.*) Me father. He has a big stick. (*She has a drink: then, whimpering as* **Mommo** *might.*) I wanta go home, I wanta go home. (*New tone, her own, frustrated.*) So do I, so do I. *Home.* (*Anger.*) Where is it, Mommo?

The silence is now being punctuated by another car passing outside, again leaving a vacuum in its wake, making the place lonelier.

A lot of activity tonight. And all weekend.

She picks up her book and does not open it. She starts to pace the periphery of the room.

'There is the silence of copse or croft
When the wind sinks dumb.
And of belfry loft
When the tenor after tolling stops its hum.
And there's the silence of a lonely pond
Where a man was drowned . . .'

(*She stops for a moment or two looking at one of the sepia-coloured photographs.*)

Where a man, and his brother who went to save him were drowned. Bury them in pairs, it's cheaper.

(*Continues pacing.*)

'Nor nigh nor yond
No newt, toad, frog to make the smallest sound.
But the silence of an empty house
Where oneself was born,
Dwelt, held carouse . . .' Did we? Hold carouse.
'With friends
Is of all silence most forlorn.
It seems no power can waken it –'

Another car passes by. Her reaction to the car:

Come in! 'Or rouse its rooms,
Or the past permit
The present to stir a torpor like a tomb's.'

Bla bla bla bla bla like a tomb's. (*To the book, and dumping it.*) Is that so? Well, I don't agree with you . . . I'm going crazy. (*Then, on reflection.*) No I'm not. (*Then suddenly to **Mommo**.*) Wake up *now*, Mommo. Mommo! Because I don't want to wait till midnight, or one or two or three o'clock in the morning, for more of your – unfinished symphony. (*She switches on the light.*) Mommo, the cursèd paraffin! (*She switches on the radio.*) What else did your father say when you gave him the story? (**Mommo** *is awake.*) What about the snails? What about the earwigs?

Mommo   'Oh never step on a snail,' he intoned.

Mary   'Nor upon the silver trail he leaves behind.'

Mommo   'For your boot is unworthy. The snail knows his place,' and understands the parameters,' (says he), 'D'yeh consider,' says he, 'that God designed all this for the likes of the gobshite Bochtáns and their antics? No freedom without structures,' he said.

Mary   On with the story! That man and his decent wife the same did as was proper on entering John Mahoney's.

Mommo   Sure we weren't mean't to be here at all!

Mary   The customary salutation was given.

Mommo   That was one of God's errors.

Mary: 'God bless all here!' – though quietly, for they were shy people, and confused in their quand'ry. Mommo? And then, without fuss, the man indicated a seat in the most private corner.

Mommo   An' they were wrongin' them there again! So they wor.

Mary   They were.

Mommo   The whispers bein' exchanged were *not* of malevolent disposition. Yis! – to be sure! – that woman! – maybe! – had a distracted look to her. Hadn't she reason?

Mary   The Bochtáns gawpin' at them.

Mommo   They knew no better.

Mary   Where would they learn it?

Mommo Oh ho, but he bet ('beat') them, he bet the best of them! (*Absently asking.*) Cigarette. 'An' I caught Tom playin' with the mangler the other evenin', his feet dancin' in the cup.' That's what she was whisperin'. And he lookin' round, 'Not at all, not at all,' tryin' to look pleasant in the house of another. 'An' won't they have to light the lamp?' that's what she was whisperin'. 'Not at all, not at all,' still lookin' for the place to put his eyes. 'Isn't Mary a big girl now an' well able to look after them.' That's what he was whisperin'. 'And won't May Glynn be lookin' in on them.' But she'd told May Glynn that mornin' not to be waitin', her mother'd be needin' her to look after her young brothers, an' they'd be home before dark for sure. And-sure-she-was-gettin'-on-his-nerves! Till he had to go an' leave her there to a quiet spot at the counter . . . Sure she should've known better. An' she's sorry now. She is. She is. (*She's beginning to whimper, puffing on the cigarette* **Mary** *has given her.*) I wanta go home, I wanta see mah father.

Mary *coming to comfort her.*

Mommo Shtap! (*Warning* **Mary**.) And he has a big stick. And he won't try to stop me telling my nice story.

Mary (*a realisation: to herself*)   . . . No, I'm not trying to stop you. 'Why doesn't she finish it and have done with it.' (*A* **Dolly** *line from earlier.*)

Mommo (*becomes conscious of the cigarette*)   What's this?

Mary (*taking cigarette from her*)   I'm not stopping you!

Mommo An' who asked for this?

Mary And I just had an idea.

Mommo } Me mouth is burned.

Mary We'll do it together!

Mommo Rubbishy cigarettes – spendin' money on rubbishy cigarettes –

Mary   And if we finish it, that would be something, wouldn't it? –

Mommo *lapses into silence, she grows drowsy, or feigns drowsiness.*

Mary   Don't go to sleep, and don't be pretending to either. 'And what'll you be havin'?' says John Mahony the proprietor. But the stranger now was taking in the laughter and Costello's great bellow dominating over all. 'A lotta noise an' little wool as the devil says shearin' the pig!' sayin' Costello, 'Wo ho ho!' 'An' what'll you be havin', mister?' says John Mahony again. 'A little drop of whiskey an' a small port wine.' And readying the drinks, says John: 'The f-frost is determined to make a night of it?' 'Behell I don't know,' says old Brian, like the nestor long ago, 'comin' on duskess there was a fine roll of cloud over in the west and if you got the bit of a breeze at all I'm thinkin' you'd soon see a thaw.' And the stranger had produced his purse and was suspended-paused takin' in the forecast. But the two little smiles appearing again: such good fortune as a thaw was not to be. Then – and with a deft enough flick – he pitched the coin on the counter, like a man rejecting all fortune. Good enough. He took the drink to his decent wife and was for sitting next to her again but wasn't her head now in and out of the corner and she startin' the cryin'.

Mommo   She should have known better.

Mary   So what could he do but leave her there again?

Mommo   An' the church owed him money.

Mary   Did it?

Mommo (*growls*)   The-church-owed-him-money. Oh, the church is slow to pay out, but if you're givin', there's nothin' like money to make the clergy fervent.

Mary   Yes?

Mommo (*drowsily*)   And I'm thinkin' that decent man of late was given to reviewin' the transpirations since his birth . . .

But if he was itself, wasn't his decent wife the same? . . . At the end of her tether . . . They were acquainted with grief. They wor . . . Switch off that aul' thing there's nothing on it (the radio) . . . They wor.

Mary (*has turned the volume down*)   Mommo?

Mommo *is asleep. The silence again.*

Mary   . . . Alright, I won't just help you, I'll do it for you. (*Progressively she begins to dramatise the story.*) Now John Mahony. (*She corrects her pronunciation.*) Now John *Mah'ny* – was noticing the goings-on between the two and being the proprietor he was possessed of the licence for interrogating newses. And 'You have ad-distance teh-teh go, mister?' says he at the stranger. An' says Grandad. An' says the stranger, class of frownin': 'Would that big man down there be a man by the name of Costello?' And, 'Th-that's who he is,' says John, 'd'yeh know him?' 'No,' says the stranger, in curious introspection, an' 'No' says he again, *still* puzzled in the head. 'But that's a fine laugh.' 'Oh 'tis a f-fine laugh right enough,' says John, 'hah?' Knowin' more was comin' but hadn't yet reached the senses. And the stranger now drawin' curlicues with his glass upon the counter! Then says he, 'I heard that laugh a wintry day two years ago across the market square in Ballindine an' I had t'ask a man who he was.' 'Yeh had,' says John, 'I had,' says the stranger. An' John was in suspense. And then of a suddenness didn't the frown go disappearin' up the stranger's cap. He had it at last. 'Well,' says he – Oh, lookin' the merchant between the two eyes, 'Well,' says he, 'I'm a better laugher than your Costello.' What time is it? *Someone* will come yet. *'Nother* supa tea. (*Short laugh to herself as she gets another glass of vodka.*) Well, I'm a better laugher than your Costello. (*She swallows the drink.*) Now the merchant betrayed nothing. He was well-versed in meeting company, an' all he did was nod the once – (*She nods.*) – and then, quick enough of him, referred the matter. And 'Sh-Sheamus!' says he, 'Sh-sh-Sheamus!' callin' Costello to come down.

She is now listening to the 'putt-putt' of the motorcycle approaching.

A mortal laughing competition there would be.

She is now into action, putting away her glass, switching off the radio, getting needle, thread, scissors and the skirt of her 'going-away' suit to take in the waist.

Dolly. Again! I wonder why. (*Cynically.*) Bringing tidings of great joy.

Dolly *comes in. She stretches herself (she has had sex in a ditch, doorway, old shed or wherever.) She takes in the packed suitcase but as usual leaves such baiting topics until it suits her.*

Dolly   I have it all figured out.

Mary   The County Home?

Dolly   Well, maybe nothing as drastic as that. That's a nice suit.

Mary (*does not lift her head from her work*)   Kill her?

Dolly (*a sideways twist of the head – 'Kill her?' – a more feasible suggestion*)   Can I have a drop of this (vodka)?

Mary   You brought it.

Dolly (*produces two bottles of mixers*)   I forgot the mixers earlier. In my haste. (*She pours two drinks.*) We might as well have a wake, an American wake for yeh.

Mary   Not for me. I had a little one earlier, thank you.

Dolly   You had *two* little ones. (*Puts drink beside* **Mary**.) Vodka and white. It's a long time since I seen you wearing that.

Mary   Saw.

Dolly   What?

Mary   I wore it coming home.

Dolly   Did you have to let out the waist?

Mary   I have to take *in* my things. (*A gesture of invitation.*)
You need to talk to someone.

Dolly   Go on: cheers! Since you're off. Are yeh?

Mary (*does not drink, does not look up but lifts her glass and puts it
down again*)   Cheers!

Dolly   And it often crossed my mind the years Stephen and
I were here with herself. Kill her. And it wouldn't be none of
your fancy nurses' potions either. Get them out of bed, the
auld reliable, start them walkin'. Walk the heart out of them.
No clues left for coroner or Dr Paddy. And that's how many's
the one met their Waterloo. What's the matter?

Mary *shakes her head; just when she does not want to, she is about
to break into tears.*

Dolly   . . . What? . . . Joking! . . . I have it all figured out.

Mary *is crying.*

Dolly   What's the matter?

Mary   Stop it, Dolly.

Dolly   Mary?

Mary   Leave me alone. (*To get away from* **Dolly** *she goes to the
radio and switches it on.*)

Dolly   What's the – Why are you? (*She emits a few whimpers.*)
Mary?

Mommo (*has woken up*)   What's the plottin' an' whisperin'
for?

Dolly   Good man, Josie! (*And immediately back to* **Mary**
again.) What? (*Crying.*) . . . Don't. Please. (*Her arms around*
Mary.)

They are all speaking at once. **Mary** *and* **Dolly** *crying.*

Mommo   Oh yes, 'Good man, Josie.' Now! Good man, Josie. And that was the second greeting he uttered that night.

Dolly   What's the matter? . . . Shh! . . . What?

Mary   I don't know, I don't know.

Mommo   He got no reply. Nor did he expect one. For Josie was a Greaney, an' none was ever right in that fambly.

Mary   I wanted to come home.

Dolly   What?

Mary   I had to come home.

Mommo   Though some say he had the knack of mendin' clocks, if he had.

Mary   This is our home.

Dolly   What?

Mary   This is *home*?

Dolly   I know it is.

Mary (*pulling away from* **Dolly** *to shout at* **Mommo**)   Finish it, finish it, that much at least!

Mommo   Ho-na ho gus a haa haa! (*Defiantly.*)

Mary   Have done with it! – that much at least!

Mommo   Heh-heh-heh-heh!

Mary (*to* **Dolly** *who is following her*)   Why don't you take off your coat!

(*To* **Mommo**.) What was waiting for them at dawn when they got home in the morning?

Mommo   Who ho ho, heh-heh-heh – Howandever. 'How the boys!' was Costello's third greeting. This time to two old men with . . . (*Etc.*)

And, again, **Dolly** *is coming to* **Mary** *to offer comfort, to be comforted, both of them crying.* **Mary** *goes to the radio and violently turns up the volume while the lights are fading and a car passes by outside.*

Act Two

An announcement for the Sunday Concert *on the radio together with* **Mommo**'s *voice continuing her story.*

She has arrived at and is repeating the last section of the story where **Mary** *left off in Act One.*

A sniff from **Mary**, *her tears are all but finished. Both she and* **Dolly** *have their 'vodkas and white' and a slice of the birthday cake on plates beside them.*

Mommo   And the stranger now drawin' curlicues with his glass upon the counter! Then says he, 'I heard that laugh a wintry day two years ago across the square in Ballindine an' I had t'ask a man who he was. 'Yeh had,' says John, 'I had,' says the stranger. An' John was in suspense.

A car passes by outside.

What time is it? Miss!

Mary   Seven. (*Then, to* **Dolly**.) I'm sorry for (crying).

Dolly   Ar – Phhh – don't be silly. Did yeh see the helicopter on Friday? The plant, they say, is for closure. The Chinese are over.

Mary   Japanese. (*Her attention now returning to* **Mommo**.)

Dolly   I prefer to call them Chinese.

Mommo   An' then of a suddenness didn't the frown go disappearing up the stranger's cap. He had it at last. 'Well,' says he – oh lookin' the merchant between the two eyes – 'Well,' says he, 'I'm a better laugher than your Costello.'

Dolly's *mind beginning to tick over on how to present her 'proposition' to* **Mary**. **Mary**'s *nervous energy, after the lull, setting her to work again, removing the bed-warmer from the fire and slipping it into the bed at* **Mommo**'s *feet, wrapping up the cake in tin foil and putting it away . . . but, predominantly, her eyes, concentration, returning to* **Mommo**; *a resoluteness increasing to have* **Mommo**'s *story finished.*

Dolly   I must get a set of decent glasses for you the next time I'm in town.

Mommo   Now the merchant has betrayed nothing. He was well-versed at meeting company. And all he did was nod the once. (*She nods solemnly.*)

Dolly   And I'm sure there's rats in that thatch.

Mommo   Then, quick enough of him, referred the matter.

Dolly   I could see Halligan the contractor about slatin' it.

Mommo   An' 'Sh-Sheamus!' says he. 'Sh-Sh-Sheamus!' Calling Costello to come down.

Dolly   What d'yeh think?

Mary   Shhh!

Mommo   A laughing competition there would be.

Dolly (*puzzled by* **Mary**'s *behaviour*)   And I was thinking of getting her a doll.

Mary   I want her to continue.

Dolly   What?

Mary   She's going to finish it.

Dolly   Finish it? Why?

Mary   I don't know. I can't do anything the way things are.

Dolly   Sit down. I thought you were trying to stop her.

Mary   She's going to finish it.

Dolly   You're always on your feet –

Mary   *Tonight!*

Dolly   Another drink?

Mary   No. A laughing competition there *will* be! (*And goes to* **Mommo**.) Then down steps the bold Costello.

Mommo Pardon?

Mary Then down steps the bold Costello.

Mommo Oh yes.

Dolly Well, as a matter of fact, I do have a proposition.

Mary Shhh!

Mommo Then down steps the bold Costello. And 'Hah?' says he, seeing the gravity on the proprietor's mien. But the proprietor – John, to be sure – referred him like that. (*She nods in one direction.*) An' 'Hah?' says Costello, lookin' at the stranger. But weren't the eyes of the stranger still mildly fixed on John, an' 'Hah?' says Costello, lookin' back at John. But there was no countin' John's cuteness. He takes the two steps backwards, then the one to the sidewards, slidin' his arse along the shelf to 'scape the stranger's line of vision an' demonstrate for all his neutrality in the matter. 'Hah?' poor Costello 'gain. 'Hah?' to the one, 'Hah?' to the other. 'Hah?' 'Hah?' The head near swung off his neck, an' now wonderin' I'm sure what on earth he'd done wrong.

Dolly Mary? (*Topping up the drinks.*)

Mommo An' no help from John. Puffing a tuneless whistle at the ceiling! 'Phuh-phuh-phuh-phuh.' (*John's tuneless whistle.*)

Mary (*absently accepting drink*) Phuh-phuh-phuh-phuh.

Dolly (*to herself*) Jesus! She's gone loopey too.

Mommo Then says the stranger, lookin' straight ahead at nothing – 'How d'yeh do, Mr Costello, I'm Séamus O'Toole.' Costello: 'Hah?! I'm very well, thanking you!' His face was a study. An' 'Oh,' says John of Costello, 'he's a Sh-Sheamus too, phuh-phuh-phuh-phuh.'

Dolly Phuh-phuh-phuh-phuh.

Mommo 'I know that,' says the stranger, 'but I'm a better laugher than 'm.' 'Quawk awk-awk-awk?' in Costello's throat. In response didn't the stranger make serious chuckle. And in response didn't Costello roar out a laugh.

Dolly   Jesus! (*She decides to take off her coat and see what effect flaunting her pregnancy will have.*)

Mary (*encouraging* **Mommo**)   Good girl! (*Silently with* **Mommo**.) Then loud as you please . . .

Mommo   Then loud as you please, says Costello: 'He says, he says, he says,' says he, 'he's a better.' (*She claps her mouth shut.*) An' that was far as he got. For in the suddenness of a discovery he found out that he was cross. 'Ara phat?' says he – He was nimble? – The full size of him skippin' backwards, the dancing antics of a boxingman. An' lookin' 'bout at his supporters, now hushed an' on their marks, 'He says, he says, he says,' says he, 'he's a better laugher than me!' What! Sure they never heard the likes. Nor how on earth to deal with it. An' the upset on their own man's face! – Oh, they war greatly taken 'back. Oh they wor. An' not up to disseration things war lookin' dangerous.

Dolly   She's getting tired – the creature.

Mary   } Shhh!

Dolly   Cheers!

Mary   Cheers – Things were looking dangerous.

Mommo   Oh, they wor.

Mary   'Ary give me (a) pint outa that.'

Mommo   Costello?

Mary *nods.*

Mommo   Swivellin' an' near knockin' them wor behind him, but then in retraction comes wheelin' back 'round, the head like a donkey's flung up at the ceilin', eyes like a bull-frog's near out their sockets an' the big mouth threwn open. But God bless us an' save us, all the emission was (a) class of a rattle'd put shame to a magpie.

Mary (*silently, excited*)   Shame to a magpie.

Mommo   Now he was humbled, the big head on him hangin', went back to his corner, turned his back on all present. The hump that was on him! Oh his feelin's wor hurted. (*She yawns:*) Oh ho hun-neo!

Mary   Aa no!

Mommo (*insistent*)   Oh ho hun-neo!

Mary   Don't be pretendin', you had a little nap a while ago.

Mommo   Put the sup of milk there for me now for the night.

Mary   I'll get the milk later. And the others, Mommo?

Mommo   Lookin' wildly, one to the other, from their giant to the stranger, none knowin' what to do.

Dolly (*getting the milk*)   Let her settle down.

Mary   But they were vexed.

Mommo   An' they knew it?

Mary *nods agreement and encouragement.*

Mommo   Oh they knew they were cross. An' strainin' towards the stranger like mastiffs on chains, fit to tear him asunder.

Dolly   And I don't know if you've noticed, Mary, but the turf out there won't last the winter. (*Approaching with the milk.*) Here we are! I'll see to the turf.

Mary (*takes the milk from* **Dolly**)   No milk.

Dolly   What are you at?

Mary   No milk! (*She puts it away.*)

Mommo   And even Josie! – the odd one –

Dolly (*to herself*)   Jesus Josie! –

Mommo   That always stood aloof! Even he was infected with the venom (that) had entered, an' all of the floor was 'vailable round him he began to walk circles screechin' 'Hackah!' at the stranger.

Dolly   I want to have a talk!

Mary   Later.

Dolly   A plan, a proposition.

Mary   Later!

Mommo   Pardon?

Dolly   I've a little problem of my own.

Mary   I think I've noticed. Go on, Mommo, no one is stopping you.

Mommo   Where's the milk for the night, miss?

Mary   Then striding to the stranger – Costello: 'Excuse me there now a minute, mister –'

Dolly   Mary –

Mary   No! No! 'Excuse me there now a minute now –'

Mommo   Pardon?

Mary   'But what did you say to me there a minute ago?'

(*Waits for a beat to see if* **Mommo** *will continue*.) . . .

'That you're a better laugher than me, is it?' . . . 'Well, would you care to put a small bet on it?'

Mommo (*suspiciously, but childlike*)   How do you know that?

Mary   Oh, I was told. But I never heard all of the story.

Mommo   Hah? . . . Ar shurrup ('shut up') outa that.

Mary   'Well would you care to put a small bet on it?' And 'No,' saying the stranger going back to his wife. 'But you're challenging me, challenging me, challenging me, y'are!'

Mommo   'No,' saying the stranger, ''twas only a notion,' his eyes on the floor. For why? Foreseeing fatalistic danger. Then joined the two little smiles cross the width of his mouth which he gave up to the hero as evidence sincere that he was for abnegating. Can yeh go on?

Mary   No. (*Cajoling.*) Can you?

Mommo   Well, Costello was for agreein'? An' for understandin'? But th' others wor all circlin', jostlin', an' pushin' – 'He is, he is, challe-gin' yeh, he is!' 'Up Bochtán, up Bochtán, Bochtán for ever!' Putting confusion in the head of Costello again. But the stranger – a cute man – headin' for the door, gives (the) nod an' wink to Costello so he'd comprehend the better the excitation (that) is produced by the abberation of a notion. Then in the fullness of magistrature, 'Attention!' roaring Costello, 'Attention!' roaring he, to declare his verdict was dismissal, an' decree that 'twas all over.

Mary   Yes?

Mommo   An' 'twas.

Mary   Aa, you have more for me?

Mommo (*childlike*)   Have I?

Mary *nods.* **Mommo** *thinking her own thoughts, then she shakes her head.*

Mary   A laughing competition there would be.

Mommo (*absently*)   A what?

Dolly   She's exhausted.

Mary   She's not!

Mommo   Where was I? . . . In the jostlin' an' pushin' . . . (*Then her eyes searching the floor, in half-memory, lamenting trampled sweets.*) The sweets.

Mary   Here they are. (*The ones that* **Dolly** *brought.*)

Mommo   No. The sweets. (*Her eyes still searching the floor.*) In the jostlin' an' pushin' . . . The sweets for her children trampled under their boots.

Dolly   Can't you see she's –

Mary   She's not!

Mommo   Phuh: dust.

Mary   But if Costello decreed 'twas all over, how did it start up again?

Mommo   How did? The small stranger, I told yeh, goin' out to check the weather for as had been forecasted the thaw was setting in.

Mary   I see!

Mommo   An' sure they could have got home.

Mary   I see!

Mommo   They could have got home. (*Brooding, growls; then.*) Costello could decree. All others could decree. But what about the things had been vexin' *her* for years? No, a woman isn't stick or stone. The forty years an' more in the one bed together (and) he to rise in the mornin' (and) not to give her a glance. An' so long it had been he had called her by first name, she'd near forgot it herself. Brigit . . . Hah? . . . An' so she thought he hated her an' maybe he did, like everything else . . . An'. (*Her head comes up, eyes fierce.*) 'Yis, yis-yis, he's challe'gin' ye, he is!' She gave it to the Bochtáns. And to her husband returning? – maybe he would recant, but she'd renege matters no longer. 'Hona ho gus hah-haa!' – she hated him too.

Mary *and* **Dolly** *are silenced: they have not heard this part of the story before.*

Mary   . . . And what happened then?

Mommo   An' what happened then. Tried to pacify her. (*Growls.*) But there-was-none-would-assuage-her. An' what happened then, an' what happened then. 'Stand up then,' says Costello. They already standin'. '*Scath siar uaim*' to the rest to clear back off the floor. The arena was ready.

Mary   And what happened then?

Mommo   An' what happened then? . . . Tired, tired.

Mary   Mommo?

Mommo (*savagely*)   Shthap! Tired! What's your business here? There are no newses here for anyone about anything.

Dolly   It's ten to ten, so your father'll hardly come now, so off with yeh to sleep. There's the good girl, and we'll hear your confession again tomorrow night. There, there now. (*To* **Mary**.) That was a new bit. There, there now . . . She's in bye-byes.

Mary   She's not.

Dolly   She's asleep! Mommo? . . . Ten to ten, 1984, and I read it – how long ago was it? – that by 1984 we'd all be going on our holidays to the moon in *Woman's Own*.

Mary   She's not asleep.

Dolly   I'm not arg'in' about it. She's – resting.

Mary   And I'm going to rouse her again in a minute. You were saying?

Dolly   And a telly would fit nicely over there.

Mary   A plan, a proposition, you have it all figured out?

Dolly   And I'm sorry now I spent the money on the video. No one uses it. You'd make more use of it. It has a remote. (*In answer to* **Mary**'s *query 'remote'*.) Yeh know? One of them things yeh – (*hold in your hand*) – and – (*further demonstrates*) – control.

Mary   I have a video here already (Mommo). What's your plan?

Dolly   Wait'll we have a drink. She's guilty.

Mary Guilty of what?

Dolly I don't know.

Mary Then why –

Dolly I'm not arg'in' with yeh! (*Offering to top up* **Mary***'s drink.*)

Mary Why can't you ever finish a subject or talk straight? I don't want another drink.

Dolly I'm talking straight.

Mary What's on your mind, Dolly? I'm up to you.

Dolly There's no one up to Dolly.

Mary Tck!

Dolly I'm talkin' straight!

Another car passes by outside.

Traffic. The weekend-long meeting at the computer plant place. And all the men, busy, locked outside the fence.

Mary (*abrupt movement to the table*)   On second thoughts. (*And pours lemonade into her glass*.)

Dolly (*is a bit drunk and getting drunker*)   No, wait a minute.

Mary What-are-you-saying, Dolly?

Dolly An' that's why she goes on like a gramophone: guilty.

Mary This is nonsense.

Dolly And so are you.

Mary So am I!

Dolly An' you owe me a debt.

Mary What do I owe you?

Dolly *And* she *had* to get married.

Mary (*to herself*)   Impossible.

Dolly   No! No! – Mary? Wait a minute –

Mary (*fingers to her forehead*)   Dolly, I'm –

Dolly   I'm talkin' straight.

Mary   Trying to get a grip of – Ahmm – I'm trying to find – ahmm – Get control of – ahmm – my life, Dolly.

Dolly   Yes. You're trying to say make head and tail of it all, talk straight, like myself. No, Mary, hold on! You told me one thing, I'll tell you another. D'yeh remember the pony-and-trap-Sunday-outings? I don't. But I remember – now try to contradict this – the day we buried Grandad. Now I was his favourite so I'll never forget it. And whereas – No, Mary! – whereas! She stood there over that hole in the ground like a rock – like a duck, like a duck, her chest stickin' out. Not a tear.

Mary   What good would tears have been?

Dolly   Not a tear. And – *And!* – Tom buried in that same hole in the ground a couple of days before. Not a tear, then or since. Oh I gathered a few 'newses' about our Mommo.

Mary   Maybe she's crying now.

Dolly   *All* of them had to get married except myself and my darling mother-in-law, Old Sharp Eyes. But she bore a bastard all the same. Her Stephen. (*She switches off the radio.*)

Mary   Leave it on.

Dolly   I've a proposition.

Mary   It's the *Sunday Concert,* switch it on.

Dolly (*switches on the radio*)   So what d'yeh think?

Mary   About *what?*

Dolly   The slated (*Gestures 'roof'.*), the other things I mentioned.

Mary It would stop the place falling down for someone alright.

Dolly An' half of this place is mine, I'll sign it over.

Mary To whom?

Dolly To *whom*. To Jack-Paddy-Andy, to Kitty-the-Hare, to you. And there might be – other things – you might need.

Mary What else could anyone possibly need?

Dolly *now looking a bit hopeless, pathetic, offering a cigarette to* **Mary**, *lighting it for her.*

Dolly An' would you like another (drink)?

Mary *shakes her head.*

Dolly Lemonade?

Mary No. What are you trying to say?

Dolly An' the turf out there won't last the winter.

Mary You said that.

Dolly And one of the children.

She looks at **Mary** *for a reaction. But all this time* **Mary**'*s mind, or half of it, is on* **Mommo**.

Dolly Yeh. Company for yeh.

Mary I get all this if I stay.

Dolly Or go.

Mary What? . . . You want me to go? With one of the children? . . . *Which* one of the children?

Dolly (*continues with closed eyes through the following*) Jesus, I'm tired. A brand new one.

Mary *laughs incredulously, high-pitched.*

Dolly Would you? Would you? Would you?

Mary   What?

Dolly   Take him. It.

Mary   With me?

Dolly (*nods*)   An' no one need be any the wiser.

Mary   And if I stay?

Dolly   Say it's yours. It'll all blow over in a month.

Mary   You're crazy.

Dolly   That makes three of us. I'm not crazy, I'm – as you can see.

Mary   Yes, I've wondered for some time, but I thought you couldn't – you couldn't! – be that stupid.

A car passes by outside.

Dolly   More take-aways for the lads. (*She starts wearily for her coat.*) My, but they're busy.

Mary   No one is asking you to leave.

Dolly (*stops. Eyes closed again*)   You'll be paid.

Mary   I've heard you come up with a few things before, but!

Dolly   Stephen'll kill me.

Mary   What about me?

Dolly   Or he'll cripple me.

Mary   Do you ever think of others!

Dolly   Or I'll fix him.

Mary   And you'll be out – gallivanting – again tomorrow night.

Dolly (*blows her top*)   And the night after, and the night after! And you can be sure of that. (*And regrets blowing her top.*)

Mary   . . . How long are you gone?

Dolly   Five, six months.

Mary   Five, six months.

Dolly   Trying to conceal it.

Mary   Who's the father?

Dolly   I have my suspicions.

Mary   But he's busy perhaps tonight, picketing?

Dolly   Yes, very busy. Travelling at the sound of speed. But the Chinese'll get them.

Mary   And this is the help? This is what you've been figuring out?

Dolly   You can return the child after, say, a year. If you want to.

Mary   I thought your figuring things out were about –? (*She indicates* **Mommo**. *Then she goes to* **Mommo**.) Mommo, open your eyes, time to continue.

Dolly   After a year it'll be easy to make up a story.

Mary   *Another* story! (*She laughs, high-pitched – there's hysteria in it.*)

Dolly   You're a nurse, you could help me if you wanted to.

Mary   Trying all my life to get out of *this* situation and now you want to present me with the muddle of your stupid life to make *sure* the saga goes on.

Dolly   Oh the saga will go on.

Mary   Mommo!

Dolly   I'll see to that, one way or the other.

Mary (*to herself*)   I go away with a brand new baby. Mommo! (*To* **Dolly**.) Where! Where do I go?

Dolly *nods.*

Mary You have that figured out too?

Dolly We can discuss that.

Mary *laughs.*

Dolly You're its aunt.

Mary Its! (*She laughs.*)

Dolly Aunt! – Aunt! – Aunt!

Mary Mommo! I know you're not asleep.

Dolly (*shrugs*) Okay. (*Now talking to herself.*) And if it's a boy you can call it Tom, and if it's a girl you can call it Tom.

Mommo Supa milk, where's the milk?

Mary Later. To continue. Where had you got to?

Mommo But in the jostlin' an' pushin'. (*Eyes searching the floor.*) The sweets . . . the sweets . . .

Dolly But I've discussed something with someone. 'Cause if I don't get Stephen, Stephen'll get me. But I know now how to get him and that's what got me saving, of late. I've made the preliminary enquiries. That little service of fixing someone is available – 'cause it's in demand – even round here. I've discussed the fee with someone.

Mommo Phuh: dust.

Mary (*to* **Dolly**) Have you finished?

Dolly (*intensely*) You had it easy!

Mary I had it easy? No one who came out of this – house – had it easy. (*To herself.*) I had it easy.

Dolly You-had-it-easy. The bright one, top of your class!

Mary (*to herself*) What would you know about it?

Dolly Top marks! – Hardly had your Leaving Cert and you couldn't wait to be gone.

Mary   I won't deny that.

Dolly   You can't! State Registered Nurse before you were twenty –

Mary   Twenty-one –

Dolly   A Sister before you were twenty-five, Assistant Matron at the age of thirty.

Mary   And a midwife?

Dolly   Yes, SRN, CMB, DDT!

Mary   All very easy.

Dolly   Couldn't get away fast enough.

Mary   But I came back, Dolly.

Dolly   Aren't you great?

Mary   I failed, it all failed. I'm as big a failure as you, and that's some failure.

Dolly *is stopped for a moment by* **Mary**'s *admission.*

Mary   You hadn't considered that?

Mommo *has started rambling again, repeating the last section of the story which she told earlier, down to 'The arena was ready'.*

Mommo   An' sure they could have got home. They could have got home. Costello could decree . . . (*Etc.*)

Dolly (*her voice over* **Mommo**'s)   No! No! You had it easy! – You had it – You had – I had – I had ten! – I had a lifetime! – A lifetime! – here with herself, doin' her every bidding, listenin' to her *seafóid* ('rambling') gettin' worse till I didn't know where I was! Pissin' in the bed beside me – I had a lifetime! Then the great Stephen – the surprise of it! – comes coortin'! Never once felt any – real – warmth from him – what's wrong with him? – but he's my rescuer, my saviour. But then, no rhyme or reason to it – He could've got a job at that plant – but he couldn't wait to be gone either! Then waitin' for the hero, my rescuer, the sun shining out of his hundred-and-thirty-five-pounds-a-week arse, to come home at Christmas. No interest in me – oh, he used me! – or in children, or the rotten thatch or the broken window, or Conor above moving in his fence from *this* side. I'm fightin' all the battles. Still fightin' the battles. And what d'yeh think he's doin' now this minute? Sittin' by the hearth in Coventry, is he? Last Christmas an' he was hardly off the bus, Old Sharp Eyes whisperin' into his ear about me. Oooo, but he waited. Jesus, how I hate him! Jesus, how I hate them! Men! Had his fun and games with me that night, *and* first thing in the morning. Even sat down to eat the hearty breakfast I made. Me thinkin', still no warmth, but maybe it's goin' to be okay. Oooo, but I should've known from *experience* about-the-great-up-standin'-Steph-en-evrabody's-fav-our-ite. Because, next thing he has me by the hair of the head, fistin' me down in the mouth. Old Sharp Eyes there, noddin' her head every time he struck an' struck an' kicked an' kicked an' pulled me round the house by the hair of the head. Jesus, men! (*Indicating the outdoors where she had sex.*) You-think-I-enjoy? *I-use-them!* Jesus, hypocrisy! An' then, me left with my face like a balloon – you saw a lot of me last Christmas, didn't yeh? – my body black and blue, the street angel an' his religious mother – 'As true as Our Lady is in heaven now, darlin's' – over the road to visit you an' Mommo with a little present an' a happy an' a holy Christmas now darlin's an' blessed St-fuckin'-Jude an' all the rest of them flyin' about for themselves up there.

Mommo   The arena was ready. A laughing competition there would be. (*She coughs in preparation.*)

Dolly   Jesus, how I *hate*! I hate her (Mommo) – I hate this house – She hates you – I hate my own new liquorice-allsorts-coloured house –

Mary (*ashen-face, shaking her head*)   No . . . No.

Dolly   She! – She! – She hates you!

Mary   No.

Dolly   And I hate you!

Mary   Why?

Dolly   Why? You don't know terror, you don't know hatred, you don't know desperation! No one came out of this house had it easy but you had it easy.

Mommo *has unwrapped a sweet and is sucking it*.

Mary   Dolly, stop it at once!

Dolly   'Dolly, stop it at once.' Look, go away an' stay away.

Mary   Dolly!

Dolly   'This is our home' – You'll need a few bob. I'll give it to you, and my grand plan: I'll look after things here, all fronts, including lovee lovee Mommo, an' Stephen'll never raise a finger to me again.

Mary   You're –

Dolly   Am I?

Mary   You're –

Dolly   Am I? We'll see – Hah! – if I'm bluffing.

Mary   Have you finished ranting?

Dolly   Ooh, 'ranting'!

Mary   You're spoilt, you're unhappy, you're running round in circles.

Dolly   *I'm* running round in circles? Suitcase packed – How many times? Puttin' on airs – look at the boots, look at the lady! You're stayin', you're goin', 'I need to talk to someone' – Fuck off! 'I wanted to come home, I had to come home' – Fuck off!

Mary   Stop it this moment, I won't have it! You're frightening her.

In reply to 'frightening her', **Dolly** *indicates* **Mommo** *who is sucking a sweet, lost in her own thoughts. Then* **Dolly** *turns her back to* **Mary**; *she continues in quieter tone.*

Dolly   The countryside produced a few sensations in the last couple of years, but my grand plan: I'll show them what can happen at the dark of night in a field. I'll come to grips with my life.

Mary   Shtaaap!

Short silence. **Mommo**'s *eyes fixed on* **Mary**.

Mommo   Miss? . . . Do I know you?

Mary *shakes her head, 'No'; she is afraid to speak; if she does she will cry.*

Mommo   . . . Pardon?

Mary *shakes her head.*

Dolly (*to the fire*)   I'll finish another part of this family's history in grander style than any of the others.

Mary   . . . The arena was ready.

Mommo   'Twas.

Mary   But Costello's laugh wasn't right at all.

Mommo   Then ''Scuse me a minute,' says he lickin' his big mouth, puts a spit in the one hand, then one in the other, an' ponders the third that he sent to the floor. (*Coughs.*) 'A wuff.'

Dolly   A wuff, wuff!

Mommo   'A wuha wuha wuha wuha, a wuha huha huha hoo, quawk awk-awk-awk a ho ho ho, a wo ho ho ho ho ho ho!' An' twasn't bad at all. Was it? An' Costello knew it. An' by way of exper'ment, though 'twasn't his turn, had a go at it again, his ear cocked to himself.

Dolly   We filled half that graveyard. Well, I'll fill the other half.

Mommo   Then, ''Scuse me too,' says the stranger makin' Costello stiffen, an' 'Heh heh heh, heh heh heh, heh heh heh,' chuckled he.

Dolly   Heh heh heh, heh heh heh, heh heh heh –

Mary (*ferociously at* **Dolly**)   Shhhtaaaap!

Mommo   . . . Miss?

Mary (*to* **Mommo**)   . . . No, you don't know me. But I was here once, and I ran away to try and blot out here. I didn't have it easy. Then I tried bad things, for a time, with someone. So then I came back, thinking I'd find – something – here, or, if I didn't, I'd put everything right. And tonight I thought I'd make a last try. Mommo? Live out the – story – finish it, move on to a place where perhaps, we could make some kind of new start. Mommo? I wanted to help you.

Dolly   And yourself.

Mary   And myself.

Mommo   Where's the milk for the night?

Mary *nods that she will get it.*

Mommo   Tck!

Mary (*to* **Dolly**)   She may hate me, you may hate me. But I don't hate her. I love her for what she's been through, and she's all that I have. She doesn't understand. Do you understand, Dolly? Please . . . And I'm sorry.

Dolly (*drunkenly*)   For what?

Mary (*turns away tearfully*)   I'm not the saint you think I am.

Dolly   The what? Saint? That'd be an awful thing to be. 'Wo ho ho, ho ho ho!'

Mommo   Yis. Did ye hear? The full style *was* returnin' an' like a great archbishop turnin' on his axis, nods an' winks to his minions that he knew all along. The cheers that went up in John Mah'ny's that night!

Now. Then. And.

'Yeh sold all your cargo?' Costello roarin' it like a master to friken a scholar. The laugh from his attendants, but then so did the stranger.

'Where (are) yeh bound for?' – stern Costello – 'Your destination, a Mhico?'

'Ballindineside, your worship.'

'Ballindineside, a Thighearna!'

'Cunn ether iss syha soory.' (*Coinn iotair is saidhthe suaraighe.*)

Dolly   Hounds of rage and bitches of wickedness!

Mommo   An' the description despicable more fitting their own place.

Dolly (*to the fire, almost dreamily*)   Why the fuck did he marry me?

Mommo   'A farmer?' says Costello. 'A goose one,' says the stranger. An' t'be fair to the Bochtáns they plauded the self-denigration.

Dolly   I don't hate anyone.

Mommo   'An' yourself?' says the stranger. 'Oh now you're questionin' me,' says Costello, 'An' rabbits,' screeches Josie, 'Hull-hull-hull, hull-hull-hull!'

Dolly (*stands*)   What did I get up for?

Mommo   An' 'Rabbits!' says the stranger. 'Rabbits?!' saying he. 'Well, heh heh heh, heh heh heh, heh heh heh, heh heh heh!' 'What's the cause of your laughter?' Costello frownin' moroya (*mar dhea*, 'as if' – *pretending seriousness*) 'Bunny rabbits!' says the stranger – 'is *that* what you're in!'

'Not at all, me little man,' says Costello, 'I've a herd of trinamanooses in Clash back the road.'

'Tame ones?' says the stranger.

'Tame ones, what else, of a certainty,' says Costello, 'an' the finest breed for 'atin' sure!'

'But for the Townies though for 'atin',' says the stranger, most sincerely. An' not able to keep the straight face, Costello roared out a laughter, an' gave beck to his attendants to plaud the stranger's cleverality.

Dolly   Where's the flashlamp?

Mommo   An' the contrariety an' venom was in it while ago!

Dolly   I want to go out the back.

Mommo   'Twas like the nicest night ever.

Dolly *makes a plea for help*.

Mommo   But they'd yet to find the topic would keep them laughin' near for ever.

Mary   Topic?

Mommo   Then one'd laugh solo, the other'd return it, then Costello'd go winkin' an' they'd both laugh together, a nod from the stranger, they'd stop the same moment to urge riotous chorus, give the others a chance.

Dolly   Don't want the fuggin' flashlamp. (*Then, as if driving cattle out of the house, she goes out the door.*) How! – How! – Hup! – Skelong. Bleddy cows! Howa-that-how! Hup! Hup! . . .

Mary   What topic did they find?

Mommo   But there can be no gainsayin' it, Costello clear had the quality laugh. 'Wo ho ho, ho ho ho': (in) the barrel of his chest would great rumbles start risin', rich rolls of round sound out of his mouth, to explode in the air an' echo back rev'berations. An' next time demonstratin' the range of his skill, go flyin' aloft (to) the heights of registration – 'Hickle-ickle-ickle-ickle!' – like a hen runnin' demented from the ardent attentions of a cock in the yard after his business. Now!

Mary And what about Grandad?

Mommo Who?

Mary The stranger.

Mommo Not much by way of big sound?

Mary No.

Mommo Or rebounding modulation?

Mary No.

Mommo But was that a stipulation?

Mary No.

Mommo He knew the tricks of providence and was cunning of exertion. Scorn for his style betimes?

Mary *nods*.

Mommo But them wor his tactics.

Mary And he was the one most in control.

Mommo He was. (*She yawns.*) Huh ho honeo.

Mary No, Mommo – It *is* a nice story – And you've nearly told it all tonight. Except for the last piece that you never tell.

Mommo Who was that woman?

Mary What woman?

Mommo Tck! – The woman just went out the door there. (*Mimicking* **Dolly**.) 'Hup-hup-howa that!'

Mary That was Dolly . . . Dolly.

Mommo An' does she always behave that way?

Mary Sometimes.

Mommo (*thinking about this; it does not make sense to her. Then eyes scrutinising* **Mary**: *in this moment she is possibly close to recognising* **Mary**) . . . Who are you?

Mary   Try a guess. Yes, Mommo? – Yes, Mommo? – Please – who am I?

Mommo   Here she is again!

Dolly *comes in. She looks bloated and tired. She wolfs down the slice of cake which she deliberately resisted earlier. Then looking for her bag, putting on her overcoat, etc.*

Dolly   And I've been starving myself.

Mommo (*whispering*)   She'd eat yeh out of house an' home . . . Is there something you require, Miss, that you're rummaging for over there?

Dolly   Your pension.

Mommo   Oh it's time for ye both to be going – ten to ten. He doesn't like calling when there's strangers in the house.

Mary   We're off now in a minute. What was that topic again that kept them on laughing?

Mommo   Misfortunes. (*She yawns.*)

Mary   Mommo? (**Mommo**'s *eyes are closed.*)

Dolly (*to herself, looking at the door*)   I hate going home.

Mary   Mommo?

Mommo (*very tired*)   Tom is in Galway. I bet him with nettles. Mitchin' from school. D'yeh think he remembers?

Mary (*gently*)   No.

Mommo   Well, I don't remember . . . I don't remember any more of it . . . (*She's asleep.*)

Mary *is defeated.*

Dolly   . . . What were you trying to do with her?

Mary   'Twas only a notion. She's asleep.

Dolly   Maybe she'd wake up again?

Mary (*slight shake of her head, 'No'*)   Sit down.

Dolly   What're yeh goin' to do?

Mary (*slight shake of her head, a tremulous sigh*)   Ahmm.

Dolly   Back to the nursing?

Mary   No. That wasn't me at all. And no confidence now anyway. (*She collects up a few odds and ends and puts them in the suitcase.*) Who's looking after the children?

Dolly   Maisie Kelly. They're stayin' the night in her house.

Mary (*absently*)   The nicest night ever.

Dolly   . . . What were we doin' that night?

Mary   Ahmm. The shade on that light: do you mind if I? (*She switches off the light and lights a candle.*) We let the fire go out. The cursèd paraffin.

Mary *has collected up a silver-backed hairbrush and a clothes brush.*

Dolly   . . . But if you're not going back to the nursing?

Mary   There must be *some* future for me, somewhere. (*She is brushing the back of* **Dolly**'s *coat.*) I can certainly scrub floors.

Dolly (*a little irritably*)   What're you doin'?

Mary   Just a little – dust – here.

Dolly   Who cares?

Mary   It's just that people talk at the slightest.

Dolly   Do you care what people say?

Mary   I'm afraid I do. There. I can't do a thing for you, Dolly. Can you lend me a hundred quid?

Dolly *nods.* **Mary** *switches off the radio.*

Mary   Well, that's it then.

Dolly *is just sitting there and* **Mary** *is standing: two figures frozen in time. Then a cortege of cars approaching, passing the house (at comparatively slow speed).*

Dolly   The funeral. The weekend-long meeting at the plant is over. Now are they travelling at the sound of speed?

Mary *laughs – titters.*

Dolly   I told you the Chinese'd get them!

Mary *laughs.* **Dolly** *joins in the laughter.* **Dolly** *now flaunting herself, clowning addressing her stomach, the bulge:*

Dolly   Good man, 'Josie'! . . . And you're 'Josie's' aunt!

They laugh louder, the laughter getting out of hand . . . until they collapse together on the floor.

Good man, Josie! . . . (*Uproariously.*) Jesus, misfortunes!

Then the unexpected: **Mommo** *is awake. She is laughing to herself*

Mary (*in a whisper*)   Shh, Dolly, shhh! (*And waits, frozen.*)

Mommo   Yis. Did ye hear? Explosions of laughter an' shouts of hurrahs! For excess of joy.

Dolly   Jesus, I'm tired. (*And titters.*)

Mary   Shh, Dolly, shhh! (*And waits, frozen.*)

Mommo   An' didn't he ferret out her eyes to see how she was farin', an' wasn't she titherin' with the best of them an' weltin' her thighs. No heed on her now to be gettin' on home. No. But offerin' to herself her own congratulations at hearin' herself laughin'. An' then, like a girl, smiled at her husband, an' his smile back so shy, like the boy he was in youth. An' the moment was for them alone. Unaware of all cares, unaware of all the others. An' how long before since their eyes had met, *mar gheal dhá gréine* ('as the light of two suns'), glowing love for each other? Not since long and long ago.

Dolly   'S alright, 's alright, Mommo: I'm Dolly, I'm like a film star. (*She lies on the bed perhaps.*)

Mommo   But now Costello's big hand was up for to call a recession. 'But how,' says he, 'is it to be indisputably decided who is the winner?' And a great silence followed. None was forgettin' this was a contest. An' the eyes that war dancin', now pending the answer, glazed an' grave in dilation: 'Twas a difficult question. (*Quietly.*) Hona ho gus hah-haa! Tired of waiting male intelligence, 'He who laughs last,' says she.

An' 'cause 'twas a woman that spoke it, Costello was frikened, darts class of a glance at her an' – (*She gulps.*) 'That's what I thought,' says he.

But wasn't that his mistake? ever callin' the recession an' he in full flight. 'Cause now, ready himself as he would, with his coughin' an' spittin', the sound emanating from a man of his talent, so forced and ungracious, he'd stop it himself.

(*Whispering.*) 'He's lost it,' says someone. (*Her derisory shout on the night.*) Hona ho gus hah-haa! (*Whispering.*) 'He should never have stopped.' Their faces like mice.

An' he'd 'tempt it an' 'tempt it an' 'tempt it again. Ach an fear mór as Bochtán (*But the big man from Bochtán*) in respiratory disaster is i ngreas casachtaí (*and in bouts of coughing*). (*She coughs . . .*) The contest was over.

Mary   The contest was over?

Mommo   Oh the strangers'd won.

Mary   But what about the topic?

Mommo   Hah?

Mary   Would keep them laughing near for ever.

Mommo (*whispers*)   Misfortunes . . . She supplied them with the topic. And it started up again with the subject of potatoes, the damnedable crop was in that year.

'Wet an' wat'rey?' says the stranger.

'Wet an' wat'rey,' laughing Costello.

'Heh heh heh, but not blighted?'

'No ho ho, ho ho ho, but scabby an' small.'

'Sour an' soapy – Heh heh heh.'

'Yis – ho ho,' says the hero. 'Hard to wash, ladies, hard to boil, ladies?'

'An' the divil t'ate – Heh heh heh!'

But they were only getting into their stride.

'An' the hay?' says old Brian, 'behell.'

'Rotted!' says the contestants, roarin' it together.

'The bita oats,' shouts young Kemple, 'Jasus!' Lodged in the field. An' the turf says another. Still in the bog, laughed the answer, an' the chickens the pip, pipes up the old crone.

An' the sheep, the staggers, an' the cow that just died, an' the man that was in it lost both arms to the thresher, an' the dead.

Mary   . . . And the dead, Mommo? Who were the dead?

Mommo   Skitherin' an' laughin' – Ih-ih-ih – at their nearest an' dearest. Her Pat was her eldest, died of consumption, had his pick of the girls an' married the widdy again' all her wishes. The decline in that fambly, she knew the widdy'd outlast him. She told them the story – an' many another. An' how Pat had come back for the two sheep (that) wor his – An' they wor – An' he was her firstborn – but you'll not have them she told him. Shy Willie inside, quiet by the hearth, but she knew he'd be able, the spawgs of hands he had on him. 'Is it goin' fightin' me own brother?' But she told him a brother was one thing, but she was his mother, an' them were her orders to give Pat the high road, and no sheep, one, two or three wor leavin' the yard. They hurted each other. An' how Pat went back empty to his strap of a widdy, an' was dead within a six months. Ih-ih-ih. (*The 'Ih-ih-ih'* *which punctuate her story sound more like in-grown sobs rather than laughter.*) She made great contributions, rollcalling the dead. Was she what or 'toxicated? An' for the sake of an auld ewe stuck in the flood was how she lost two of the others, Jimmy and Michael. Great gales of laughter following each name of the departed. Ih-ih-ih. An' the nice wife was near her time, which one of them left behind him?

Mary   Daddy.

Mommo   Died tryin' to give birth to the fourth was to be in it. An' she herself left with the care of three small childre waitin'. All contributions receiving volleys of cheers . . . Nothin' was sacred an' nothing a secret. The unbaptised an' stillborn in shoeboxes planted, at the dead hour of night treading softly the Lisheen to make the regulation hole. Not more, not less than two feet deep. And too fearful of the field, haunted by infants, to speak or to pray. They were fearful for their ankles – Ih-ih-ih. An' tryin' not to hasten, steal away again, leaving their pagan parcels in isolation forever. Ih-ih-ih. And Willie too, her pet, went foreign after the others. An' *did* she drive them all away? Never ever to be heard of, ever again. Save Willie, aged thirty-four, in Louisaville Kentucky, died, peritonitis. The nicest night ever, that's what I'm sayin'. And all of them present, their heads threwn back abandoned in festivities of guffaws: the wretched and neglected, dilapidated an' forlorn, the forgotten an' despairing, ragged an' dirty, eyes big as saucers ridiculing an' defying of their lot on earth below – Glintin' their defiance of Him – their defiance an' rejection, inviting of what else might come or *care* to come! – driving bellows of refusal at the sky through the roof. Hona ho gus hah-haa! . . .

Mary   I see.

Mommo   I want to see my father.

Mary   I see.

Mommo   But they'd soon get their answer.

Mary   Who would?

Mommo   The Bochtáns, the Bochtáns sure! Tck!
Mauleogs drunk?

Mary *nods.*

Mommo   Them all packed together?

Mary *nods.*

Mommo   The foul odour that was in it, you'd hardly get
your breath. The two contestants sweating, the big man most
profusely – Sure they'd been contending the title now five or
six hours. An' Costello, openin' down his shirts an' loosenin'
his buckle, was doublin' up an' staggerin' an' holdin' his
sides. 'Aw Jasus, lads, ye have me killed – Hickle-ickle-ickle,'
an' the laughing lines upon his mien wor more like lines of
pain. An' the stranger 'Heh heh heh heh, heh heh heh heh,'
aisy an' gentle. Then beholding his 'ponent, his complexion
changin' colours the frown came to his brow bringin' stillness
upon him an' the two little smiles to the sides of his mouth.
Suddenly he shouts, 'Costello's the winner!' But sure they
wouldn't have it – nor herself in the corner. 'He's nat ('not'),
he's nat, he's nat, he's nat!' 'On, on-on, Bochtán for ever!'

'No-no! – Heh-heh – he has me bet!'

'He's nat, he's nat, he's nat, he's nat!'

The others, 'Up Bochtán! Bochtán for ever!'

An' Costello now all the while in upper registration –
'Hickle-ickle-ickle-ickle' – longin' to put stop to it, his own
cacklin' wouldn't let him. An' 'deed, when he'd 'tempt to rise
an arm – an' sure he wasn't able – in gesture of cessation, th'
others mistakin' of his purpose would go thinkin' t' do it
for'm ('for him') puncturin' holes in the ceilin', batin' stomps
on the floor.

An' the stranger now could only stand and watch. An' late it
was herself realised the Great Adversary had entered.

'Hickle-ickle-ickle-ickle, Aw Jasus, lads, I'm dyin'.' Then slow in a swoon he went down to the floor. For the last moments were left him 'twas the stranger that held him, for there was nothing now in the world to save him or able to save him.

Mary   And what's the rest of it? Only a little bit left.

Mommo (*musing*)   For there was nothing now in the world to save him . . .

Dolly   Mary?

Mary   You're going to be alright, Dolly. Roll in under the blanket.

*She helps **Dolly** get under the blankets.*

Mommo   . . . Or able to save him. Did I not say that bit? Oh yis. 'An' the rabbits, lads,' says Cost'llo, 'I didn't sell e'er the one of them, but threwn them comin' home for fun again' Patch Curran's door.' And that was the last he was to utter that night or any other.

Mary   They don't laugh there anymore.

Mommo   Save the childre, until they arrive at the age of reason. Now! Bochtán for ever is Bailegangaire.

*Through the following **Mary** puts away her suitcase, tidies some things away, undresses behind the headboard and puts on a simple nightdress, and gets the cup of milk for **Mommo**.*

Mary   To conclude.

Mommo   Yes. They wor for lettin' them home, d'yeh know? Home without hinder. Till the thief, Josie, started cryin' at death, and was demanding the boots be took of the stranger to affirm 'twas feet or no was in them. An' from trying to quieten his excitation someone of them got hit. Then he struck back. Till they forgot what they wor doin' sure, or how it had started, but all drawin' kicks an' blows, one upon the other, till the venom went rampant. They pulled the stranger down off the cart an' gave him the kickin'. Oh they gave him such a doin', till John Mah'ny an' the curate (that) was called prevailed again' the Bolsheviks.

'Twas dawn when they got home. Not without trepidation? But the three small childre, like ye, their care, wor safe an' sound fast asleep on the settle. Now, my fondlings, settle down an' be sayin' yere prayers. I forget what happened the three sticks of rock. Hail Holy Queen –Yes? Mother of Mercy – Yes? Hail our lives? – Yes? Our sweetness and our hope.

Mary   It was a bad year for the crops, a good one for mushrooms, and the three small children were waiting for their gran and their grandad to come home. Mommo? My bit. Mary was the eldest. She was the clever one, and she was seven. Dolly, the second, was like a film-star and she was grandad's favourite. And they were in and out of the road watching for the horse and cart. Waiting for ribbons. And Tom who was the youngest, when he got excited would go pacing o'er and o'er the boundary of the yard. He had confided in Mary his expectation. They would be bringing him his dearest wish – Grandad told him secretly – a mouth organ for Christmas. That was alright. But in the – excitation – of their waiting they forgot to pay attention to the fire. Then Mary and Dolly heard – 'twas like an explosion. Tom had got the paraffin and, not the careful way Grandad did it, shhtiolled it on to the embers, and the sudden blaze came out on top of him. And when they ran in and . . . saw him, Mary got . . . hysterical. Then Mary sent Dolly across the fields for May Glynn. And sure May was only . . . eleven? Then Mary covered . . . the wounds . . . from the bag of flour in the corner. She'd be better now, and quicker now, at knowing what to do. And then May Glynn's mother came and they took Tom away to Galway, where he died . . . Two mornings later, and he had only just put the kettle on the hook, didn't Grandad, the stranger, go down too, slow in a swoon . . . Mommo?

Mommo   It got him at last.

Mary   Will you take your pills now?

Mommo   The yellow ones.

Mary   Yes.

Mommo   Poor Séamus.

She takes the pills with a sup of milk.

Mary   Is there anything else you need?

Mommo   To thee do we cry – Yes? Poor banished children of Eve.

Mary   Is there anything you have to say to me?

Mommo   Be sayin' yere prayers now an' ye'll be goin' to sleep. To thee do we send up our sighs – Yes? For yere Mammy an' Daddy an' Grandad is (who are) in heaven.

Mary   And Tom.

Mommo   Yes. An' he only a ladeen was afeared of the gander. An' tell them ye're all good. Mourning and weeping in this valley of tears. (*She is handing the cup back to* **Mary**.) And sure a tear isn't such a bad thing, Mary, and haven't we everything we need here, the two of us. (*And she settles down to sleep.*)

Mary (*tears of gratitude brim to her eyes*)   Oh we have, Mommo.

She gets into the bed beside **Mommo**. **Dolly** *is on the other side of* **Mommo**.

Mary   . . . To conclude. It's a strange old place alright, in whatever wisdom He has to have made it this way. But in whatever wisdom there is, in the year 1984, it was decided to give that – fambly . . . of strangers another chance, and a brand new baby to gladden their home.

Schubert's 'Notturno' comes in under **Mary**'s *final speech.*

Tom Murphy

A Thief of a Christmas

The actuality of how Bailegangaire came by its appellation

A Thief of a Christmas was first produced at the Abbey
Theatre, Dublin in December 1985, with the following cast:

Brian	Paul Bennett
Stephen	Michéal Ó Briain
John's Wife	Bríd Ní Neachtain
Bina	May Cluskey
Josie	Garrett Keogh
Costello	Mick Lally
John	Peadar Lamb
Martin John	Macdara O Fatharta
Anthony	Darragh Kelly
Tomás Rua	Dónall Farmer
Peggy	Eithne Dempsey
Stranger	Bob Carlile
Stranger's Wife	Joan O' Hara

Community: Niall O'Brien, Joy Forsythe, Eleanor Feely, Sarah
Carroll, Michelle O'Connor, Anne Enright, Marie Sutton,
Joan Fogarty, Helen Nugent, Deirdre Herbert, David
Herlihy, Niall O'Keefe, Patrick Brady, Paud Murray, Conday
Conarain, Michael O'Doherty, Ray Cooke, Noel O'Donovan,
Bill Cowley, Lorraine Bond

Children: Nell Murphy, Eoin Sharp, Elaine Grace, Martin
Lynch, Jane O'Reilly

Musicians: Michéal Mac Aogáin, Michéal O Briain, Antoin
Mac Gabhann

Director Roy Heayberd
Settings & Costumes Chisato Yoshimi
Lighting Tony Wakefield
Musical Director Micheal Mac Aogain
Fight Director Mark Shelley

Characters

Brian
Stephen
John's Wife
Bina
Josie
Costello
John
Martin John
Anthony
Tomás Rua
Peggy
Stranger (*Séamus from* Brigit, *Mommo's husband*)
Stranger's Wife (*Mommo from* Brigit *and* Bailegangaire)

Others: villagers; child; a fiddler and a melodeon player (the musicians can be male or female, or one of each sex)

Place: A pub-cum-general store in a remote village.

Time: About 30 years ago.

Act One

*Christmas is a matter of days away. It is about six o'clock and darkness has fallen. Oil lamps light the pub-cum-general store. Groceries, sweets, items of clothing and hardware, **John**'s cubby-hole of an office (which is also, probably, the post office) at the end nearest the front door. At the other end of the rough counter is the pub. Here we have an open fire, timber forms and timber 'half' barrels provide the seating; a low ceiling. A door behind the counter leads to the kitchen and living quarters. All quite primitive. We are dealing with a neglected, forgotten peasantry.*

*Two old men, **Brian** and **Stephen**, are seated by the fire, pints beside them. A **Fiddler** in a corner is putting resin on his bow. But it is on **John's Wife**, Rose, a young buxom woman in her twenties, that the lights come up. She is attending a customer at the shop end, entering items in a ledger.*

John's Wife   Six tallow Christmas candles for to put in your windows, a pair of black laces for your Sunday boots, a fine-tooth comb, a half-a-pound of black puddin'. (*She stoops to pick up a **Child** who has started to whinge, hidden behind the counter.*) And what else was there?

*The customer she is attending to is **Bina**, a crone, dressed in a mixture of traditional clothing and the gaudy cast-offs of a girl. A bandage over one eye.*

Bina   The laxatives.

John's Wife   He's going to kill himself eating them laxatives.

Bina   None can stop him, he thinks they're sweets and will have nothing else.

John's Wife   You're too good to him. Now: tobaccy, icing sugar, raisins, Bex tartar – Isn't it very quiet, Bina? Matches.

Bina   And the salt, ma'am.

John's Wife   Them all away at the Big Market. (*Writing:*) S.A.L.T. But the roads are bad for them getting home. And was there anything else you required?

Bina   The usual drop of –

She leaves it unfinished, another musician is entering – an **Accordionist** (*can be a man or a woman*).

John's Wife   You're back again for us this year, Kate/Willie!

Accordionist   And I had the time of it getting here. How are ye all?

John's Wife   Grand! McDonagh (*the* **Fiddler**) is waitin' ablow (*below*) for yeh.

The **Accordionist** *joins the* **Fiddler**.

John's Wife   We'll have the night of it.

Bina   We will as always. And the singing!

John's Wife   And the dancing! An' what were yeh saying?

Bina   The naggin of brandy.

John's Wife (*conspiratorially*)   Oh yes. We'll have the roolyeh-boolyeh, we will, in faith! And I never seen more stuff leave Bochtán for fair or market than I did this morning. Now, the brandy, and here's a drop to warm you up for now. Throw that back yeh. (*And she, too, has a secret drink for herself.*) An' 'twill be a blessin' after that bad harvest.

Bina (*drinks; then concerned*)   But was I right do you think to give poor Tufty to Michael O'Donoghue to sell for me?

John's Wife (*dandling the* **Child**)   Deedydle-um deedydle – And what else did you have to sell but the cow?!

Bina   But without himself knowing?

John's Wife   And won't you have money in your purse tonight like the others comin' home?

Bina   But he's lucid at times and gets cross.

John's Wife   Keep givin' him the laxatives. (*Writing:*)
Brandy. As much as he can eat of them.

*Outside, someone (***Costello***) is arriving on a bicycle, calling out
a greeting.*

Costello's Voice   There y'are, Josie!

John's Wife   Whist! Is that . . .?

Costello's Voice   Diabolically cold!

John's Wife   Knuck-kaw och-khaw, Costello is back!

Bina   Costello, och-khaw!

John's Wife   Now things'll start livenin' up in earnest –
knuch-kaw och-khaw!

Bina   Och khaw a-khaw!

Josie *comes in.*

Bina   Josie.

Josie *is the eccentric one; in middle thirties, skinny and severe-
looking. Unlike the others who are dressed against the weather in
layers of rough clothing, his dress is sparse. Shirt open at the neck,
threadbare jacket and trousers, yet showing no effects of the cold
weather. He is carrying his spade and a switch (or cane).*

John's Wife   How yeh, Josie, is that Costello arriving?

Josie (*ignoring them, uttering his severe nasal sound*)
Heh-hinnia!

Bina   Yeh didn't, Josie, think to bring my clock?

But **Josie** *has continued to the pub end of the shop to do his annual
party piece.*

John's Wife   Pleb! (*Calls.*) John!

Bina*'s eyes continuing after* **Josie***, then an imploring glance at*
John's Wife*.*

John's Wife   Oh he has it mended, all knows the *amadán*
('fool') has it mended these three days.

Bina (*has taken a few timid steps after* **Josie**)   Because with the money I'll have from the sale of Tufty, you can charge me what you like, almost.

Josie (*warning her to keep away*)   Heh-hinnia!

Because she is interfering with the business – his 'performance' – which he is now engaged in.

John's Wife   Look at him! Ride-the-Blind-Donkey, year after year. Leave him so (for) a while till he has a few pints and suitably placated, then I'll get John to speak to him. (*Calls.*) John! (*To* **Bina**.) Give me your pension book.

Bina   I think he has it (the clock) in his pocket.

John's Wife   Ludráman ('Idiot') (Josie is)! Your pension money now is for last week's and I have them articles down with the others that are outstanding.

Bina   That will do, ma'am (I understand).

And during this **Josie** *has commenced his party piece: he bridges the gap between two half-barrels with the spade, produces four flowers (or thistles) from his pocket and sets them erect, spaced apart, two on each barrel; then, standing astride the handle of the spade, he blindfolds himself; then, sitting on the spade handle, his two feet off the ground; then, maintaining this delicate balance, he urges on his 'donkey'; then, at some point, he makes four deft flicks of his switch taking the heads off the four flowers. His performance completed, he removes the blindfold, sets up four more flowers on the barrels and invites all present to have a go.*

Josie   Heh-hinnia?! . . . (*Quiet, sour satisfaction, to himself.*) Hin-ma-a-a-ay!

And he goes to the counter to rap severely on it. His performance receives very little attention from the others present. The musicians conferring and playing trial snatches of music for themselves; a single philosophical groan from **Stephen** *to the fire – as his remarks throughout.*

Stephen   Oh yis!

Costello *enters before* **Josie***'s performance is completed. He is a fine big man, a bit overweight, in his late thirties. The main feature of his character is his great laugh. As is frequent in gatherings there is someone with an unusual-sounding laugh, an infectious laugh.* (**Costello***'s laugh explodes in the air – a great rumble – before going flying up into a cackling falsetto.*) *Indeed, even at a distance, when people see or hear him approaching, an involuntary gurgle of laughter starts in their throats.*

Costello   Cold enough for ye, ladies!

Bina   Khaw och-khaw, Séamusheen a wockeen, God bless you!

John's Wife   Knuck-uck-uck-khaw, hunucka huckina-khaw, Costello!

Costello   Rose, me flower! An' fresh and well you're lookin', Bina!

Bina   Khaw-khaw-och-khaw!

John's Wife   Knuck-uck-uck hunucka-khaw!

Costello   Well, isn't it diabolically cold, ladies?

John's Wife   How was the market, Jimmy?

Costello (*evades the question*). How the man! (*To the* **Child**.) Isn't he gettin' awful big, God bless him? Jack Frost is comin' with a vengeance for you tonight – Or the Bogey Man maybe bejingoes! Well, someone is comin' anaways if you aren't good!

John's Wife   You all sold well, Jimmy?

Costello (*leaving them*)   Josie has the festivities started for us already. Good man, Josie! (To **Brian** *and* **Stephen**.) How the boys!

Brian (*a coughing, spitting gurgle*)   A hacktha, Séamus, kuh-hucht! (*As throughout.*)

Stephen   Oh yis! (*Philosophically to the fire – as throughout.*)

Costello   Diabolically cold, boys!

John's Wife (*calling again to kitchen*)   John! (*She's nasal.*)

She is outside the counter now and, with **Bina**, *coming to the pub end.*

Brian   I seen yeh – A hacktha! – early enough on the road this mornin' and I drawin' the bucket of water at the gable of the house.

Costello   Yeh did, Brian – Wo-ho-ho! – an' you had trouble crackin' the crust of ice on top of the barrel?

Brian   I had!

Costello (*his falsetto giggle*)   Hickle-ickle-ickle-ickle, you had!

Brian   Kuh-hucktha! – I had.

Stephen   Oh yis!

Costello   Well you're still the sweetest flower, Rose!

John's Wife (*harshly*)   John, will yeh come out!

Brian   An' what's the news from the Big World?

Costello   The Dutch has taken Holland!

Followed by a bellow of laughter that has the others – except **Josie** *– laughing and chuckling.*

Stephen   Oh yis!

John's Wife   But yeh sold well, Jimmy?

Costello   No, but wait'll I tell ye. Coupla miles back the road, comin' this ways to Bochtán, I seen the quarest couple. A woman in black between the two hind shafts of a cart, bent an' craite as the Linaun Shee, an' she cryin' kinda strange-like – Hah? – an' whingein' away to herself?

Bina (*whispering*)   Makin' this way?

Costello   Makin' this way, Bina.

John's Wife   Yes?

Costello   An' her man, a class of a little gadhahaun – Jasus, I nearly ran over him! Leadin' a black horse by the winkers, an' – 'Good evening' says he up at me, smilin' in the corners of his mouth.

Bina (*whispering*)   'Good evening.'

John *is entering from the kitchen chewing the last of a meal and licking his teeth. He is sixty, small, he is at least thirty years his wife's senior, he has a stammer. If all were known he is a very wealthy man. His moods can change rapidly. At the moment he is very pleased with himself and, like the others, he has great expectations of the evening and the party.*

Costello   Now, Bina, 'Good evening'. Good man, John!

John   You're here, K-Costello?

Costello   I am, John –

John's Wife   An' what was in the cart? –

Costello   Throw us out an auld pint – I'm thinkin' something white.

John (*in answer to* **Josie**'s *rapping*)   It's k-k-k-comin' Josie! Have you done your trick? (*Laughing to himself.*)

Costello   Oh he has, he has.

John   Ruh-ruh-ruh-Ride-the-Blind-Donkey. (*And laughs again.*)

Costello   An' no bother to him, boy.

Josie (*inviting challengers*)   Heh-hinnia?!

John (*giving a pint to* **Josie**)   No-no-no, there's no one to best yeh. And the first drink is on the house.

Costello   Good man, John, yeh never failed us in anything!

John (*filling* **Costello**'s *pint*)   An' whuh-what're the musicians havin'?

Costello   Whiskey.

John   An'-an'-an' as m-much, nearly, as ye can drink of it, because that's the kind of man I am!

Costello   Man, John! An' a drop of the hard tack too for me.

John (*to* **Costello**)   Bring that (whiskies) over to them. (*To his wife.*) Stoke up the fire, bring in more turf. The night that's to be in it.

John's Wife (*stoking the fire*)   A drop of brandy, Bina?

Bina   Oh no-no-no, John, no.

John   Oh n-no-no-no, John, no, but why a poor man like me, with a poor crayture of a wife like that, has t-to be standin' ye drinks, I don't know.

*He winks at his wife's bottom – perhaps pats it – for the amusement of the others. Curiously, in this case, **Costello** is not amused and his action is protective of the young woman.*

Costello   Here, Rose, let me do that: you don't know how to build a decent fire.

John's Wife *now understands what the chuckling is about.*

John's Wife   Thanks, Jimmy (*Then she glares at **John** and imitates his stammer.*) Duh-duh-duh-duh-duh! (*Defiantly gets a drink for herself; to the musicians.*) F-f-fire away! Let the p-p-party buh-buh-buh-begin!

John (*flustered for a moment*)   But-but-but, see what good the p-pensions will do ye, stuck in the mattresses when ye're all d-dead.

Costello (*when he gets his pint*)   A toast! To honest John Mahony. Drink to his health or else, says he, on the crown of yere heads, arses up in the air, sure as be damned it's in hell ye shall be!

*A rumble of laughter from **Costello**, the others chuckling, as they raise their glasses.*

John   N-not at-at-at (all). But thanks, thanks, thank ye all now.

Music continues.

You wor ('were') in ch-Tuam, K-Costello?

Costello   I was in Tuam, John.

John's Wife   You wor, Jimmy.

Costello   I was, Rose.

Bina (*smiling her expectation*)   An' how was it?

Costello   Well, not tellin' ye a word of a lie now, but 'twas deadly.

Silence.

John's Wife   Ara stop! (*Meaning that he is joking.*)

But there is no smile from **Costello**.

Bina (*an awed whisper*)   Ory!

John's Wife   Did yeh hear?

John *now tight-lipped, a frown on his brow.*

Stephen (*funereally*)   Oh yis!

John's Wife (*whispering*)   Well, d'yeh tell me so?

Costello   I do tell yeh so!

John's Wife   No.

Costello   Talkin' about a Maragadh Mor?! I never in all me born days seen likes or light of it.

John   *J-Jasus Christ!* An'-an'-an' look at all the stock I bought in for the Christmas!

John's Wife (*whispering at* **Costello**)   Yis?

Costello   Firkins of butter an' cheese be the hundredweight, says he! Ducks, geese, chickens, bonhams and! (*He claps his mouth shut.*) Geese?! Geese says he?! There was hundreds of them! There was hundreds upon hundreds of thousands of them! The ground I tell ye was white with them!

Bina (*whispers*)   White with them.

John   They went ch-cheap then?

Costello   Cheap then?!

John   Sis-sis-stop your rappin' there now, Josie, or you won't get as much as a p-p-pint of water here tonight!

Costello   Cheap then?! –

Josie (*he has the money*)   Heh-hinnia-money! –

John (*filling another pint for* **Josie**)   Ch-ch-ch-ch-cheap then – (*To* **Josie**.) Stop! – ch-cheap then, isn't that what I said? Ch-cheap then!

Costello   Sure you couldn't give them away sure!

John (*planking a pint in front of* **Josie**)   Now am I f-f-f-friggin' f-fillin' it f-fast enough for yeh?

Josie   Heh-hinnia! (*Planking down his coins.*)

Costello   Sure the sight of so many ducks an' geese an' chickens an' what-nots, sure all the people could do was stand an' stare!

Bina (*whispers*)   They were puzzled.

John *is sighing heavily through his nose, trying to think how to turn misfortune into fortune.*

John (*to musicians*)   Stop, will ye!

Costello   Can't ye play something nice an' delicate for the decent man (that) hired ye. An' the small one yeh promised me, John.

John   F-f-frig the small one!

The musicians have been conferring and now start to play 'Hard Times'.

(*To himself.*) So no one sis-sold nothin'.

Bina (*to herself*)   Aw Lord no!

Costello (*rooting in his pockets for coins*)   Oh well, if you're (**John** is) goin' back on your word. But I'm telling yeh, Napoleon Bonaparte wouldn't have said no to all the provisions goin a-begging in that town of Tuam today.

John (*irritably*)   Hah?

Costello   On his retreat from Moscow sure!

John   J-J-Jesus, I'm mythered! (*His head is confused.*)

Costello   Or Josephine – Wuw! – neither. (*And another rumble of laughter.*)

John (*angrily*)   But you sis-sold all the r-rabbits, did yeh, K-Costello?

Costello (*slight hesitation*)   Aw –

John   Aw! – Aw!

Costello   Oh, I sold, oh I did, did! – Oh, on me solemn-'n-dyin' oath, every man-jack-rabbit of them! Luck again, men!

Bina   An' Tufty?

John   Yeh-yeh-yeh codjer yeh-yeh! (*Walking away to his office, followed by his* **Wife**.)

Brian   An' who else was in it from Bochtán, Séamus?

Costello   Sure everyone, sure! The Kemples, Martin John and Anthony.

Brian   Pigs they had?

Costello   Pigs, yes, *bonavs* (bonhams).

Brian   An' Tomás Rua.

Costello   An' Tomás.

Stephen (*groans to fire, funereally*)   Cabbage plants!

Costello   Cabbage plants, to be sure, yes, what else. An' the Sheridans, the Garas, Sheehans, Mick Shlevin, Pat Shaughnessy, the O'Connors.

Bina   Michael O'Donoghue? I gave him the cow to sell for me.

Costello   I passed the two of them on the road, Michael an' Tufty. Ara what, Bina, wasn't she only a pet to yeh? Sorrier ye'd be if yeh sold her.

Brian   They'll all be here soon.

Costello   No. But home, and with heads bent, they'll be goin'.

During the above, **John's Wife** *has been whispering to* **John** *in his office at the other end of the shop;* **John** *wincing and sighing and gesturing his frustration.*

John   Look it, woman! . . . Pestered! F-f-f-frig the friggin' clock! (*But he is returning to the pub end to engage with* **Costello** *and* **Josie** *to* **Costello**.) K-k-k-codjer – you're-you're-you're only a fool – P-p-p-people laughin' at the sight of yeh!

Costello   What did I (do) – ?

John (*to* **Josie**)   An'-an' you, yeh-yeh-yeh dunce, yeh-yeh thick pleb, yeh-yeh-yeh jolter-headed gob-shite! – Give that woman back her K-clock!

Josie   Heh-hinnia!

John   K-cobblin' at it these three months –

Josie   Hinnia-whose-business? (*Whose business is that?*) –

John   The whole country knowin' you have it m-mended.

John's Wife   He has it in his pocket.

John   J-J-Jasus! – (*Catches* **Josie**.) I can hear the tick!

Bina   I miss the tick –

John   Walkin' round like a t-time-bomb! –

Josie   Heh-hinnia! – (*He has broken free.*)

Bina   I've no money to pay him now –

John's Wife   John'll pay him for yeh.

John   J-Jasus, John'll pay him! Sh-Stephen! –

John's Wife   What'll it cost but the bob or two?

John (*to* **Wife**)   Will you tend to the child! Will you speak to him, Stephen? You're his f-f-father, aren't yeh? – if y'are!

Old **Stephen** *looks up from the fire – possibly for the first time – alarmed at the suggestion of speaking to his son,* **Josie**.

Josie (*at* **Stephen**)   Heh-hinnia!

John (*en route to his office*)   Sis-sis-sort it out for yereselves then, but th-the roof is gone from over my head! (*Returning with his big ledger.*) Lookit! Not a one of ye hasn't his or her name down here in red writin'. J-Jasus every time I look at it I see the Poor House waiting for me!

John's Wife (*taking the* **Child** *into the kitchen*)   Stop your whingein' now or you'll know what you'll get from me – in there with yeh!

John (*returning*)   An'-an'-an' some of ye goin' round like buh-big ranchers – (*To musicians.*) Frig 'Moonlight in Mayo'!

The musicians stop playing 'Hard Times'.

(*To* **Costello**.) With fields to burn – Ye don't know what to do with them, overrun with weeds. The g-grandest humour till yeh came in that door, Costello, now I'd f-f-fight with St Peter!

Costello   But what did I –

John   But-but-but, K-Costello yourself! Will you sell me that field I was askin' about?

Costello   I won't.

John   Yeh won't, an' I'm expected to keep fillin' you up with porter. The village fool, you're only a scrounger, an' a scavenger. But J-J-John'll do this, J-John'll do that, John'll keep ye all g-g-g-goin!

Brian   Whist!

And they are all now listening to a cart stopping on the road outside.

Bina   Is it the strange creatures you met on the road, Séamus?

Stephen (*groans to the fire*)   'Tis the wheels of Kemples' ass an' cart.

Martin John's Voice   I'll see yeh in a minute then!

The cart moving off.

Martin John *comes in. He is in his early twenties.* (**Anthony** *who comes in later is a couple of years younger.*) *The day's disaster on* **Martin John**'s *face.*

John   You 'rived in time for the party, Martin John Kemple! Ye have yere party there now with what's in front of ye. (*He is moving off; he turns back.*) Well, I'm tellin' ye all now, a thief of a Christmas we're all goin' t'have!

He goes to his office, and stands there, his hand resting on his holy book, the ledger.

Martin John (*a muted greeting*)   Men!

Muted replies.

Costello (*sighs*)   Well, I don't know . . . One yeh sold?

Martin John   Two. (*He is counting his pittance of money.*)

Josie (*challenging* **Martin John** *to Ride-the-Blind-Donkey*) Heh-hinnia?

Costello   Stop, Josie! Give us a song, Bina. (*He winks at* **Josie**'s *back suggesting to her a song might soften* **Josie**.) Girl on yeh!

Bina starts to sing *'The Swanee River'. The musicians to accompany her. As she sings*:

Costello (*to* **Martin John**)   Try a deal with himself (**John**) for the *bonavs*, tell him you'll over-winter them for him. An' what else can we do?!

Martin John *goes to* **John** *and we see him whispering like a penitent and demonstrating on his fingers his assets and prospects. And* **Costello** *is searching the mantelpiece and looking over the counter for a pack of cards.*

Costello   Good girl, Bina! 'When I was playing with my brother!'

Right, men, Spoil Five, First Fifteen or A Hundred and Ten! Did anyone see the – Where's the pack of cards, John?

John (*calls back*)   The-the child et ('ate') them!

Brian (*whispering*)   He's not givin' them out.

Costello   But sure he didn't ate ('eat') them all?!

John *continues sighing and shaking his head to* **Martin John**. **Bina** *finishes her song. They forget to applaud her.*

Costello (*sighs*)   Well, indeed, I do not know.

Brian   Huchta-hachtha!

Josie (*quietly*)   Heh-hinnia!

Stephen   Oh yis!

Costello   . . . But *something*'ll turn up yet!

Tomás Rua, *a one-armed man, about fifty, has entered accompanied by his daughter* **Peggy**, *a comsumptive-looking girl.*

Tomás Rua   Could I see yeh in a minute for a minute, John, when you're ready? (*He signals/mimes the message*.)

He continues to the pub end where he is greeted. He merely nods in reply to the greetings; it is obvious that he is in poor straits.

Costello   Tomás!

Brian   Tomás, a mac ('son')!

Costello   And pretty Peggy! Ye'll give us a song, Peggy, in a while.

John's *eyes have shown an interest in* **Tomás Rua**; *he is eager to get away from* **Martin John** *and he has begun making his way to the pub end.*

Martin John   Aw but not for that price! –

John   Lookit – highest regard for the Kemples always but excuse me now, Martin John! (*He leaves* **Martin John**; *he gives a sweet to* **Peggy**.) Now, Peggy, that's for you. (*He gives the pack of cards to* **Costello**.) Ye'd think it was a k-k-k-casino. Yeh wanted a word, Tomás? (*Leading* **Tomás Rua** *to the office.*) D-did ye sis-see a doctor for her like I advised?

And they commence whispering and dealing at **John**'s *little office.*

Costello (*counting the cards*)   How'd yeh get on?

Martin John *sighs in frustration.*

Costello   Jasus, they're well chewed alright (the cards). And if he had my bottom field that butts his, an' the other half of Tomás Rua's little place on the other side of him . . . (*To the cards.*) Hah? Thirty-nine cards out of a pack of fifty-two! An' the best eatin' was in the hearts. (*He rejects the cards.*) We're not goin' to prosper in this diversion tonight. Oh, but the night will send us something yet, won't it, Peggy?

Anthony *is coming in backwards: he remains with his head poking out the door for a moment. The rattling and creaking of a horse and cart approaching.*

Brian   Whist!

John's Wife *enters with an armful of turf and is stopped by the silence.*

Stephen (*to the fire*)   'Tis the strangers.

Martin John   Did yeh pass them, Séamus? – The strangers.

Costello   The Linaun Shee? An' the little gadhahaun of a man with her. (*He winks at the Kemples.*)

Martin John (*peeping out the window*)   They're stoppin'. They're lookin' up at Loughran's hill.

Costello   They won't get up it.

Others peeping out the window.

Martin John   They're lookin' back the road they came.

Costello   They won't get back it. (*Winks at* **Martin John** *again.*)

Martin John   Lord Christ tonight an' Jasus, but we didn't know in the distance what at all on earth was in it, was dazzlin' in the dip ablow longside Patch Curran's place!

Costello   Even th'aul ass himself was frikened, Martin John?

Martin John   An' me thinkin' 'twas the Divil ablow, his forges started eruptin'!

Costello (*mock urgency*)   With the help of God they'll not come in here, Josie! (*At the window*). He's lookin' this way!

Costello *and* **Martin John** *are blackguarding/frightening the others, but they are also frightening themselves.*

John's Wife   But what at all in heaven or earth was dazzlin' ye?

Stephen   'Twas the showers of sparks risin' from the horse's hooves slippin'.

John's Wife   Ara stop!

Bina (*whispering*)   Maybe it was more?

Martin John   Well, I don't know – And they wor quiet, Anthony? – but the *bonavs* that were sleepin' of a sudden started screechin'.

Bina (*whispers*)   Now.

Costello   Now, Bina. A quare, strange year we had of it, and could this be the explanation?

Bina   They're roundin' the gable, goin' into the yard!

Brian   A-hacktha! Aw but ye stopped?

Costello   They were afeared not to.

Martin John   An' near destroyed pull an' pushin' horse an' cart up the hill.

John's Wife   An' who are they?

Martin John   Sure we didn't have the wind to ask them.

Costello   Nor heart after the encounter? (*Back to* **Martin John**.) Here, give me your money, I'll pool it with mine. (**Martin John** *is reluctant, wondering is he being conned, but he gives his money to* **Costello**.)

Costello   We need fortifications. (*Calls.*) John!

John *is concluding his business with the downcast* **Tomás Rua**: *a deal has not been struck, but* **John**'s *return to good form suggests that he is optimistic. They are returning to the pub end,* **Tomás Rua** *to sit beside his daughter and, unconsciously, commence thumping his knee at his plight.*

John   Th-think it over now, Tomás. No one is r-rushin' yeh. An' I always had the highest regard for your in-in-in-intelligence. (*To* **Costello**.) An' if you, yeh-yeh playboy, had the sense you'd be considerin' too what thum-thum-Tomás Rua is goin' to do.

Costello   A pint an' a small one, John, for me – The money is there! – and a pint for Martin John and Anthony.

John's Wife   There's two strangers in the yard.

John   Take that (a whiskey) over to Tomás – An' leave your knee along now, Tomás! You're goin' to do the right an' p-p-proper thing. On the house (the whiskey *is*) an'- an'-an' the bottle of minerals for that grand little daughter of his, the creature.

John's Wife   Two quare strangers –

John   I heard you. An' hoo-hoo-hoo whoever they are, an' whuh-whuh-whuh whatever they are, an' wheh-wheh-wheh –

Costello   Wherever they're goin', they'll not get there, John, the night that's in it – throw me out the small one – nor to the top of the Himalayas of India neither, not even if they had a motor car!

Stephen (*to the fire*)   You can't bate ('beat') the aul' ass all the same.

Costello   Well, here's health and bright glory to us all, and a happy and holy . . .

The strangers enter.

Well, here's to the hand that made the ball that shot Lord Leitrim in Donegal!

The strangers stand in the doorway (the back door from the yard). The **Stranger** *is in his sixties. He is wearing a cap and the usual peasant dress. There is a dignity and politeness about him; and the 'smiles' on the corners of his mouth suggest a quiet defiance of adversity as well as a fatalistic streak. His* **Wife** *is fiftyish, a black shawl over her head, falling on to and around the shoulders of an overcoat. At times when she draws the shawl about her we see that she has three sticks of rock (sweets) in her hand.*

Stranger (*quietly*)   God bless all here.

Bina (*whispering*)   What did he say?

Brian   Kuh-hacktha! (*Coughs a reply to the strangers.*)

Josie (*quietly, to himself*)   Heh-hinnia!

The **Stranger** *indicates a seat to his* **Wife** *in a corner. An involuntary sob from* **Wife***. The* **Stranger** *smiles at the locals again and nods at them.* **Costello** *and* **Martin John** *nod back.*

John's Wife   What has she in her hand?

John (*to strangers*)   God bless ye, ye're welcome! – (*To his wife.*) Sis-sweets, now d'yeh know?! (*To the others who are still gawking at the strangers.*) Have ye no m-manners? Yid (*you would*) think 'twas Ros-Roscommon people ye were!

Costello (*slagging*)   D'ye know no better?! (*Quietly to* **Josie***.*) Though I don't like it. Still, your turn, give us that song of yours, 'The Boston Burglar', Josie!

John's Wife   Sweets?

John   Sis-sis-sweets, sweets, is your curiosity satisfied now?

Costello (*raising his fresh pint*)   Luck, men! (*And he rumbles a laugh to himself.*)

The **Stranger** *registers an interest in* **Costello***, as if trying to remember something. Now he is inclining his head towards his* **Wife** *to hear the better what she is whispering.*

Stranger's Wife   And I caught Tom the other evening playing with the mangler, his feet dancin' in the cup.

Stranger   Not at all, not at all.

Stranger's Wife   And won't they have to light the lamp? The paraffin.

Stranger   Not at all, not at all.

Stranger's Wife   And the fox on the prowl, sure they'll not think to secure the hens.

Stranger   Isn't Mary a big girl now and well able to look after the other two?

Stranger's Wife   An won't they –

Stranger   Stop! . . . May Glynn'll be lookin' in on them.

Stranger's Wife   Three miles across fields.

Stranger   Or someone else then.

Stranger's Wife   And sure we told them for sure we'd be home before dark.

Stranger (*stands abruptly, betraying an inner concern and a turbulence, but he controls himself again and sits*)   Not at all, not at all. (*But he is up again and will go to the counter.*)

Overlapping the above, the locals have been continuing.

Martin John   But did yeh see all the fowl?

Costello   The cluckin' an' the quackin' an' the cacklin' of them!

Martin John   An the screechin' an' the squealin' of all the pigs in the *bonav*-market!

Costello   Oh, a lota noise an' little wool as the devil said shearin' the pig!

Another rumble of laughter. **John** *has come to serve the* **Stranger**.

John   That's a bad night outside, mister.

Stranger   It is. (*But he is listening to* **Costello** *again.*) It is, a bad night.

John   Whuh-what'll you be havin'?

Stranger   We can't get up the hill.

John   I understand.

Stranger   I put my horse and cart into one of your stables.

John   An' you're welcome.

Stranger   Till I see what to do.

John   You'll be h-havin' something?

Stranger   A small whiskey, and a drop of port wine.

John (*getting drinks*)   The frost is determined to make a night of it?

Brian   Behell I don't know: comin' on duskess there was a fine roll of cloud over in the west and if you got the bit of a breeze at all I'm thinkin' you'd soon see a thaw.

Costello   'Deed yeh won't see any thaw – What harm! 'Oh I am a bold bachelor aisy an' free, both city an' country is aiqual ('equal') to me!'

Another rumble of laughter from **Costello** *and he has the others laughing. The* **Stranger** *is listening to them.*

Anthony *has a go at Ride-the-Blind-Donkey. Ad-libs, etc.*

John *brings drinks to the* **Stranger**.

John   Now, mister.

Stranger   Thank you.

He takes the drinks to his **Wife**. **Wife** *now starts to cry, her head turned in and out of the corner.*

There is nothing the **Stranger** *can do for her so he goes back to the counter.*

John (*to* **Stranger**)   Yeh have a distance to go, mister.

Stranger   I have.

John   Yes?

Stranger (*puzzling to himself*)   Would that big man down there be a man be the name of Costello?

John   Th-th-that's who he is.

Stranger, *frowning, nods solemnly.*

John   D'yeh know him?

Stranger   No.

John   Hah?

Stranger   No. But that's a fine laugh?

John   Oh, 'tis a fine laugh right enough.

Stranger   Tis.

John   Yes?

Stranger   I heard that laugh a wintry day, two years ago, across the market square in Ballindine, and I had to ask a man who he was.

John   Yeh had.

Stranger (*nods but he is still puzzled by a thought that hasn't yet reached the senses*)   I had.

John   Yes?

Stranger   I had.

John   Yes, yeh had!

Then the **Stranger** *looks at* **John**.

Stranger   Well, I'm a better laugher than your Costello.

John's *surprise, then he nods, once, solemnly. Then he calls:*

John   K-K-K-Costello! . . . Sh-Séamus! Will yeh come down a minute.

Costello (*joining them*)   Hah? (**John** *directs his attention to the* **Stranger**.) Hah? (*But the* **Stranger**'s *eyes are still fixed on* **John**; *to* **John**.) Hah?

But **John** *refers* **Costello** *back to the* **Stranger** *again as he takes a step backwards to get out of the* **Stranger**'s *line of vision and to declare his neutrality in the matter.* **Costello**'s *head now turning from* **John** *to* **Stranger** *and growing bewildered.*

Costello   Hah? Hah? Hah? Hah?

Stranger (*eyes straight ahead*)   How d'yeh do, Mr Costello?

Costello (*to* **Stranger**)   Hah?! (*He looks at* **John**.)

John (*puffing a tuneless whistle at the ceiling*)   Phuh-phuh phuh-phuh.

Stranger   I'm Séamus O'Toole.

Costello's *head from* **Stranger** *to* **John** *again.*

John   Oh – Phuh phuh phuh – M-m-m-mister Costello's a Séamus too.

Stranger   I know that. But I'm a better laugher than'm.

Costello *gurgles an incredulous laugh in his throat.*

Stranger (*chuckles in reply*)   Heh-heh-heh-heh, heh-heh-heh-heh!

Costello (*laughing in his throat again, then breaking off to declare*)   He says, he says, he says to me, he's a better! (*He claps his mouth shut, discovering suddenly that he is angry.*) *Ara phat?!* ('What'?! *And skipping backwards and forwards like a man preparing to fight.*)

The **Stranger** *chuckles.*

Costello   He says, he says, he says to me (that) he's a better laugher than me!

The locals have never heard the likes,- nor do they know how to deal with it, so things are looking dangerous. They start to make angry sounds in their throats, not knowing quite why.

Ara, give me a pint outa that! (*As he starts back to his place, sweeping people out of his way, then changes his mind suddenly and swivels about. He sets himself squarely on his feet, head swung upwards, mouth open and utters a strange-sounding bellow. But it is forced, it has no mirth, and he claps his mouth shut, snorts in frustration and goes back to the counter, his back to the others.*)

The **Stranger** *chuckles again, this time at himself, at the outrageous idea that came into his head and he returns to his* **Wife**.

The others, glancing from one to the other, from the **Stranger** *to* **Costello** *– and seeing* **Costello**'s *upset – are making further angry* *noises. And even* **Josie**, *who usually remains aloof, does a circle of the floor, calling nasally at the* **Stranger** –

Josie   Heh-hinnia!

Costello (*holding up his empty glass*)   John! – S'alright, lads. Pint for myself, Martin John and Anthony! (*To* **John**.) S'alright, isn't it? I'll find the money for the drink. Maybe – you'd never know – we might do a deal about that bottom field of mine yet. And one for Josie! (*Starts singing.*) 'I was born an' reared in Boston, a place you all –' And one for Bina! – 'know well'. But isn't it diabolically cold, men? 'Brought up by honest parents, the truth to ye I'll tell; brought up by –' Come on, Bina! – 'honest parents and reared most tenderly, till I became –'

Josie (*singing off-key, nasally*)   'Till I became a sporting lad –'

Costello   Good girl, Bina! 'At the age of twenty-three' –

Josie   'At the age of twenty-three' –

Bina (*starts singing*) 'Way down upon the Swanee River –'

Josie   'My character was broken –'

Bina   'Far, far away –'

Costello   Oh sorry, Josie, that's your song. 'Let us pause in life's pleasures –' ('*Hard Times'.*)

Josie   'And I was sent to jail –'

Bina   'That's where my heart is longing ever –'

Costello   Good on ye, cas amach é ('throw it out')! – 'And count its many tears –'

The musicians are trying to complement. **Josie**, **Bina** *and* **Costello** *are now singing three different songs simultaneously.*

Josie   'My friends and parents did their best –'

Bina   'That's where I long to stay –'

Costello   'Hard times, hard times come again no more –'

Josie   'For to get me out on bail –'

Bina   'All the world is sad and weary –'

Costello   'Many days you have lingered –'

Josie   'But the jury found me guilty –'

Bina   'Everywhere I roam –'

Costello   'Oh hard times come again no more' – Thanks, John. (*for a fresh pint*).

Josie   'And the clerk he wrote it down –'

Bina   'Oh, darkie, how my heart grows weary –'

Costello   ''Tis the sad cry of the weary – (*A traditional compliment to the others' singing*)' Style! –

Josie   'For the breaking of the Union Bank –'

Bina   'Far from the old folks at home –'

Costello   'Hard times, hard times, come again no more –'

Josie   'I can see my dear old father standing at the door –'

Bina   'When I was playing with my brother –'

Costello   'Many days you have lingered –' (*A toast:*) Luck, men!

Josie   'Likewise my dear old mother, she was tearing out her hair –'

Bina   'Happy was I, still longing for the old plantation –'

Costello (*talking to himself, not yet discovering he is angry*)   Hah? . . . Hah?

Josie   'She was tearing out her old grey locks –'

Bina   'Still longing for the old plantation –'

Costello   'Oh hard times come again no more –'

Josie   'Crying John, my son, what have you done –'

Bina 'There let me live or die.'

Costello (*angrily to himself*)   What?!

Bina *stops.* **Costello** *is striding to the strangers.* **Josie** *continues singing for a few seconds.*

Josie 'To be sent to Charles Town . . .'

The strangers have been conferring and the **Stranger** *has risen to go out and check the weather.*

Costello   Excuse me there a minute now, but what did you say to me there a minute ago? That you're a better laugher than me, is it?

The **Stranger** *gives a silent 'No'. And is making for the door.*

Costello   No! No! – Excuse me! That you're the better laugher is it?

Stranger   No.

Costello   Well, would you care to put a small bet on it?

Stranger   No.

Costello   But you're challe'gin' me, challe'gin' me, challe'gin' me, y'are!

Stranger   No.

Martin John   He is, he is, he is, he is, he is! Look at him smilin'! –

Josie   Heh-hinnia?! –

Stranger   No! No! . . .

Costello   Hah?

John   Ary sh-sh-sh-sure you're not, mister? –

Costello   'Hat?! –

Martin John   He is, to be sure – Jasus! –

Stranger   No. –

Josie   Challe'gin – heh-hinn – yeh! –

Costello   Is it me to be afraid of yeh – or the likes of yeh – or either of ye – yeh gadahaun yeh?! –

Others (*shouting*) He is, he is, Séamus, challe'gin' yeh –

John   A-a-aisy! –

Stranger (*quietly*)   No. 'Twas only a notion. (*And he winks at* **Costello** *so that* **Costello** *will understand the better and he adds his chuckle*.) Heh-heh-heh, heh-heh-heh.

Costello *half-understanding*.

Stranger   Just goin' out to check the weather.

But a melee has started. They are milling round the strangers. **John's Wife** *and* **Child** *are out from the kitchen again*.

Others   He is, he is, Costello! –

Josie   Heh-hinnia!–

Martin John   Can't yeh hear him – 'Heh-heh-heh, heh-heh-heh'! –

John   D-Didn't the man say he's not?! –

Martin John   Stand where y'are, mister! – Jasus! –

Bina   An' bad cess to ye – an' to the two of ye! –

Martin John   Bochtán, up Bochtán, Bochtán for ever! –

John   A-aisy, a-aisy! – (*To his wife*.) Will yeh-yeh-yeh look to the child – (*To the others*.) Will ye-ye stop will ye!

Costello (*roars*)   Silence!

He throws **Josie** *back*.

Bina   The clock! (*Concerned for her clock in* **Josie**'s *pocket*.)

Costello   Till I think . . . You're not? (**Stranger** *shakes his head*.) That's alright then. My decree: it's all over.

John   An'-an' that's my decree too. N-now d'ye know?

Costello (*drinking*)   Luck men!

Stephen (*to the fire*)   Oh yis: 'tis not all over.

Now that they have returned to their places, we see the **Stranger's Wife**, *face aghast, on her knees, looking at the floor. In the jostling and pushing the three sticks of rock* (*the sweets*) *were knocked out of her hand and trampled underfoot. She picks up crumbs of the sweets and looks at them – dust.*

Stranger's Wife   The sweets! Dust.

Silence.

John   Whuh-whuh-what's up with yeh, m-ma'am?

Stranger's Wife (*whispers*)   The sweets for the children! My grandchildren! The children that were left in my care!

John   . . . Hah?

Stranger *who has been making for the door is coming back to her.*

Stranger (*helping her to her feet*)   Shhhh!

Stranger's Wife (*shakes off his hands; shouts*)   Hona-ho 'gus hah-haa!

Stranger   Shh, woman!

Stranger's Wife (*to* **John**)   You can decree! – (*To* **Costello**.) You can decree! – (*To her husband.*) All others can decree! but I'll-bear-matters-no-longer! (*To* **Costello**.) He's challe'gin' yeh, he is!

Some of them are frightened of her, including **Costello**.

(*To her husband, quietly.*) Well then? (*And she sits.*)

Costello (to **Stranger**, *who is already standing*)   Stand up then. (*To the others.*) *Scaith siar uaim* ('Get away from me')! – clear back off the floor! 'Scuse me a minute. (*He coughs in preparation.*) A-wuffa-hachkht! (*Puts a spit in one hand, then one in the other; opens* *his mouth: a sudden thought and he claps his mouth shut.*) What's the topic?

John (*to himself*)   J-Jasus Christ!

Costello   The topic to launch us . . . Then we'll have to do without one. (*He goes through the motions of preparation but claps his mouth shut again.*) Wait a minute. Who's to go first?

Martin John *tosses a coin in the air.*

Martin John (*to the contestants*)   Cry!

Costello   Harps, sure, harps.

Martin John   Harps. (*To* **Stranger**.) Heads to go first.

Stranger *looks at his* **Wife**. *She refuses to look at him.*

Stranger   'Scuse me too. (*He coughs. Then chuckles.*) Heh-heh-heh, heh-heh-heh, heh-heh-heh, heh-heh-heh!

Costello   Fair enough. (*And launches himself into it, but it is no more than a staccato-type rattle which he is not pleased with.*)

Stranger   Heh-heh-heh, heh-heh –

Costello   No, that was only a preparation.

John (*to someone*)   K-Costello's bet ('beaten')

Another attempt from **Costello**: *it is appalling.*

Stranger   Heh-heh-heh-heh, heh-heh-heh-heh.

Costello's *supporters are hushed and concerned for him.*

John   He's b-bet.

Costello *tries again: abortive.*

Stranger   Heh-heh-heh-heh, heh-heh-heh-heh!

John   B-bet. K-clown, f-fool, sis-scrounger!

Martin John (*whispering*)   Come on, Costello!

Bina (*whispering*)   Shout it out, Séamusheen!

Josie (*whispering*)   Heh-hinnia!

John   He's bet, b-bet, 'tis all over!

Costello *cues in the musicians and they start to play. He tries again: fluent laughter is returning but he truncates it or lets it die. An idea is occurring to him. The* **Stranger** *replies, his laugh is free, easy.*

John   'Tis all over, he has yeh done, k-codger yeh-yeh!

Costello *replies, fluently again at the start, – and his supporters are cheering: 'Man, Costello!' 'Up Bochtán – yahoo!' 'Hih-hinn, Costello!' But they become silent again when the laugh turns into a bout of coughing.*

Costello (*coughing*)   He has me bet, has he? Who says he has me bet?

John   Isn't it p-plain an' k-clear he has?

Costello   Is it? Will you bet on it?

John (*laughs*)   What have *you* to bet?

Costello   The back field of mine you're always talking about. What'll you bet against it?

John   Hah?

Costello   What'll you bet on him beatin' me – against the field?

John   Teh-teh-twenty pound.

Costello   Tck! Twenty pounds an' you'll give me the shop an' throw in Rose as well.

John   I'll g-give yeh g-good kick in the arse!

Costello   But isn't it plain an' clear, yeh said, I'm bet already.

John   An' y'are!

Costello   Twenty for the field if I lose, sixty-five if I win.

John   Twenty for it if yeh lose, f-f-forty if you win. (*And that's his final word.*)

Costello (*it's frustrating and unsatisfactory but he agrees*) Anyone else for a bet on the contest?

John (*to his wife*)   Write it down.

Bina   I'll bet Tufty.

Costello   The cow? Again' me, Bina! An we related on me mother's side?

Bina   What can I do, Séamus? And I'd follow John Mah'ny's head any time.

Costello   What's she worth t'yeh, Tufty?

Bina   Fifteen pounds, and win or lose, you'll have it from the money John'll give yeh.

Costello   Done!

Josie   Hennia – I'll bet the clock!

Costello   Stop, Josie, the clock isn't yours to bet.

Josie   Hinn-handiwork on it is! I'm backin' you – Heh-hinnia!

Costello   What were you goin' to charge Bina for the handiwork?

Josie   Two-hin-thruppence.

Costello   Alright. If I win you give me one and a penny-ha'penny for my trouble *and* the clock, which I'll sell to Bina for thirty bob, which she'll have from the money I give her for Tufty from what I'll get from John, win or lose, and Bina'll give you the other one an' a penny-ha'penny for your handiwork.

Josie   Hinnia-done!

Costello   Tomás? (**Tomás Rua** *shakes his head*.) Whatever he's (John is) offering for your fields, take a bit less an' back me an' you'll have your farm and the money.

John   No! All d-done now.

Costello (*to* **Tomás Rua**)   Wha'?

Tomás Rua *shakes his head*

John   An'-an'-an' you're a wise man.

Tomás Rua *mimes*, '*But I won't be shoutin' again yeh, Séamus!*'

Costello (*winks at* **Martin John**)   All done then, Martin John?

Martin John   The *bonavs*! We'll wager them on Costello, John.

John   For what I offered yeh?

Martin John   How much did yeh offer?

John   Eight pounds.

Martin John   For how many of them?

John   J-Jasus for the lot of them!

Martin John   Double it, ten if he loses.

John   You'll take ten if he wins and five if he loses. (*And he gestures 'That's it'*.)

Martin John *looks at* **Costello** *and* **Costello** *nods*.

Martin John   Done. (*He signs the book*.)

Costello   Write it all down, Rose.

Josie   Hinn – I'll bet me spade!

Costello   Stop, Josie –

Josie   Again' yeh, hinnia, this time!

Costello   Stop, you're confusing a matter that's now clear as spring water.

John   Let ye begin. (*To* **Stranger**.)

Stranger   Heh-heh-heh-heh-heh-heh-heh!

An unsatisfactory reply from **Costello**.

John   B-bet, yeh-yeh-you're bet already. (**John** *laughs*.) Stranger!

Stranger   Heh-heh-heh-heh-heh-heh-heh!

Costello *tries another laugh and is shaking his head and sighing in frustration. But he is shamming. He has thought of something further. He takes off one of his two top-coats, wearily, coughing. The book is brought by* **John's Wife** *to* **Costello** *for his signature.*

Costello (*hesitates over signing the book*)   I don't know.

John   D-don't be trying to get out of it now, yeh-yeh clown-f-fool!

Costello   Alright. Yeh stole one thing on me, John Mah'ny, but you'll never steal another.

John   What did I sis-steal on yeh?

Costello   Which way was the way to your bed, Rose?

John's Wife (*eyes cast down*)   It was through the church, Jimmy.

Costello   Was it? With the freshest featured man in Bochtán. (*To* **John**.) Forget the back field. I'm sick of being called a f-fool by you. The whole farm to you for nothing if I lose.

Silence in the pub.

Are you interested?

John   If-if yeh don't lose?

Costello   Oh, I won't lose.

Stranger   Heh-heh-heh-heh-heh!

John   F-f-f-if yeh don't lose?

Costello   I keep the farm and you'll be givin' me a hundred pounds.

John   . . . He'll bate yeh.

Costello   Oh, your little horse (**Stranger**) looks confident enough.

John   (*Yeh*) N-never wuh-won, d-did anything in your life! (**Costello** *nods.*) F-fool yeh!

Costello (*nods again*)   What's a hundred pounds to a generous man like you? Sure all you're stakin' is your happiness and a lifetime of regret.

John   K-k-codger!

Costello   Man or mouse?

John   J-Jasus Christ! – Stop! – Me head! (*His hands to his head.*)

Costello   But then, you're thinkin', how much land does a man of your age need.

John (*angrily*)   Maybe no more than a man of your age: six by two by six!

Costello   Correct.

John   Hundred pounds, so b-be it, the farm to me for n-nothing if you lose. (*He has written the bet into the book.*) Write your name there. And the book will stand.

Costello (*signs the book*)   Oh, the book will stand.

John   S-stand back now everyone. (*Give the contestants space. Gives a glass of port to his wife to take to the* **Stranger's Wife***.*) Take that over to herself, she's upsetting Costello. (*Takes a small whiskey to the* **Stranger***.*) An'-an' yeh won't leave this house empty-handed wh-when ye win.

Costello   Are we ready?

John   S-stand back everyone!

Costello   Now if we only had the topic to launch us and keep us going.

Stranger's Wife   Misfortunes.

Stranger   Whist!

Costello (*toasts* **Stranger**)   Well, here's to you, mister – bad an' all as you are!

Stranger   And to yourself – bad an' all as I am, I'm as good as you are!

Costello   We'll laugh at the music. (*He cues in musicians. His laugh is a bit forced or tentative.*) Wo-ho-ho-ho-ho!

Stranger   Heh-heh-heh-heh-heh-heh! (*Easy, fluent.*)

Costello   Wo-ho-ho-ho-ho! (*Tentative.*)

Stranger   Heh-heh-heh-heh-heh-heh-heh!

Costello (*stops the music while he drains his glass. To himself*) Why didn't I think of this in the years gone by?

He cues in the music and laughs. It is a great, rich, rumbling, resonant laugh, he lets it fly up to falsetto and brings it back again. There is wild cheering. The **Stranger** *is laughing in admiration of* **Costello**. *The music is lively. The* **Child** *is wide-eyed.*

Act Two

Before the lights come up, we hear an isolated voice in the far distance, laughing. Then another voice, calling: 'What's happening?' 'A laughing competition!' The other voice laughs: A what?' Other voices repeating the above, relaying the news to the surrounding countryside of what is going on at **John***'s, the voices growing louder until we are outside and inside the pub.*

Costello   The laughing is gone all the way to Dunmore and back!

Stranger   Heh-heh-heh-heh, heh-heh-heh-heh-heh-heh-heh!

It is two hours later. Ideally, the pub is packed and there are more people outside. (If there is room in the pub, then, perhaps, those outside are ashamed to come in, they have no money.) Those who have arrived in the last two hours are shaped and formed by poverty and hardship. Rags of clothing, deformities. But they are individual in themselves. If there is a beautiful young woman present; she, too, looks freakish because of her very beauty. The sounds of sheep, goats, sea-birds can be heard in their speech, and laughter.

Costello *is king and he knows it. He caters for his minions, those outside as well as inside the pub. He has removed his second topcoat. He is sweating.*

The **Stranger***, too, is sweating but he is, and he will continue to be, most in control.*

Josie *is nearly in hysterics.* **Martin John** *and* **Anthony** *are wide-eyed with delight; they are also counselling* **Tomás Rua** *to change his mind about putting a bet on the outcome of the contest.* **Tomás Rua** *is beginning to wonder if he should speculate.* **Bina** *is urging the* **Stranger** *to greater efforts.* **John** *is watchful. He and his wife are serving drinks.* **Brian** *coughs, 'Kuh-huchta!', and* **Stephen***, philosophically/funereally, to the fire, 'Oh yis!'*

Costello   Well, there was a man here one time – Michael Corcoran – and we'd be out at night as youngsters, throwing stones and boodhauns at his door –

Others have started to laugh, recognising the story. **Costello** *silences them.*

An' he'd be out after us, dancing with rage: 'I know ye well whoever ye are!'

Others laughing. The line being relayed to those outside.

Wo-ho-ho, wo-ho-ho . . .!

Stranger   Heh-heh-heh-heh-heh-heh-heh!

Costello.   Give us a story yourself, mister.

Stranger (*shaking his head, laughing*)   Heh-heh-heh-heh-heh-heh-heh!

Bina   Aa, God blast yeh, stranger, blast it louder back at him.

Brian   The one about Peader Bane, Séamus!

Costello   Aw, Jesus, Peadar Bane! – Wo-ho-ho! We all watching him out there one day, driving the one auld sheep – for that was all he had. And the sheep running this way and that way on Peader and, says Peader – Hickle-ickle-ickle-ickle – says Peader – Hickle-ickle-ickle-ickle! What did Peader say?

Several Voices   'It's very hard to bring one of them together!'

A great response from inside and outside. The line is celebrated in repetition. And:

Others   Man, Costello!

On, Costello! On-on-on!

Up Bochtán!

Bochtán for ever!

Josie   Hih-hinnia . . .!

Costello *is walking about majestically.* **Martin John** *and* **Anthony** *bring* **Tomás Rua** *to confer/conspire with* **Costello**, *briefly.* **Costello** *is telling them that in a little while he will pretend to be losing – he bends over sideways, like a man with a pain.*

John   Aa, come on, k-come on, is it a contest or isn't it? Letting other people do it for ye!

Costello   Wo ho ho . . .

Stranger   Heh heh heh . . .

Costello   Throw us out another pint, John!

John   It's w-waitin' for yeh, an' it's on the house. (*Gives* **Costello** *a pint.*)

The **Stranger** *is calling for a drink but* **John** *turns his back on him.* **John** *gives a glass of port to his* **Wife** *and tells her to take it to the* **Stranger's Wife**.

Costello   Well, here's to the generosity of John Mahony again!

Martin John   Aisy on the tack ('Go easy on the drink'), Séamus.

Costello (*dismissive*)   Ara what! (*Drinks.*) The gallant John Mahony over there, out courting Rose, his bride-to-be: 'There's shtars ('stars') up that side, an' there's shtars up that side!' – (*Upward movement of the cuffs of his jacket, wiping his nose.*)

Wo-ho-ho . . .!

Stranger   Heh-heh-heh . . .! A whiskey, if you please.

John   D'yeh know what you're doin'?

Bina   Or is it keepin' the throat soft y'are, mister?

John   You're pacin' yourself nicely, isn't that what you're doing?

*The **Stranger** gets his whiskey and raises his glass to **Costello**.*

Costello　An' to you an' yours again!

Stranger　An' if mine ever come across you and yours –

Costello　I hope they'll do as much for them –

Stranger　As you and yours did for me an' mine!

They laugh together. Others laughing.

John　Now, Tomás! (*He gives whiskey to **Tomás Rua**.*)

Tomás Rua *slips the whiskey to **Anthony** who slips it into the **Stranger**'s hand a few moments later.*

*Meanwhile, **Costello** is walking around the **Stranger** in silence. Then, to the **Stranger**'s back, he goes:*

Costello　Boo!

Stranger　Heh-heh-heh-heh-heh-heh-heh!

Costello　Well, you're the Devil!

Stranger (*walks around **Costello** and, to his back, he goes*) Heh-heh-heh-heh-heh-heh-heh!

John　L-laugh for laugh, K-Costello, p-play the game!

Costello　Wo-ho-ho-ho-ho-ho-ho! The Devil.

Stranger　I'm among friends then. Heh-heh-heh . . .!

Martin John　Tomás Rua wants to wager with yeh, John, after all!

John　J-Jasus Christ, ye-ye're all after John's blood! An' the tricks of ye! (*Has come outside the counter to take the drink out of the **Stranger**'s hand.*)

Martin John　Half the price you offered him if Costello loses and –

John　Heedin' scallywags (**Martin**, **John** *and* **Anthony**). An' tryin' to get this man here drunk. (*He returns the drink to*

Tomás Rua.) An'-an'-an' that little daughter of yours coughing knocks at death's door! K-come back to your place here, K-Costello! (*To* **Stranger**.) Isn't drink tomorrow to you as good as drink today! L-laugh for l-laugh now.

Costello (*returns from the doorway*)   The devil. Answer me this one, mister –

Josie   Hih-hinnia-Devil!

Costello   Stand back, Josie! Take away the 'd' an' what have you?

Stranger   Evil.

Josie   Take away – Hinnia–

Costello   Josie! Swing the 'e' around to the back an' what have yeh?

Stranger   Vile.

Costello   Vile sure, yes, vile – an' take away the 'v' an' the 'e'–

Stranger   Il.

Bina.   An' what's left without the 'i'?

Stranger   'L'.

Costello   An' that sounds very much to me like –

All   Hell! (*Laughing*.) Hell!

Costello   Hell an' damnation! – Wo-ho-ho-ho-ho-ho . . .!

Stranger   Heh-heh-heh-heh-heh-heh-heh . . .!

Costello (*clowning, turning circles*)   Let us pause in life's pleasures, he says! (*Silence. Then:*) Wo-ho-ho-ho-ho-ho-ho!

Stranger   Heh-heh-heh-heh-heh-heh-heh!

Costello   This is gettin' serious. (*Silence. Then:*) Heh-heh-heh-heh-heh-heh-heh !

Stranger.   Wo-ho-ho-ho-ho-ho-ho!

Costello (*circling, then puts his fist through the ceiling and, as if he had hurt his hand*)   Ow! Boo-hoo-hoo-hoo-hoo-hoo- hoo!

Stranger   Heh-heh-heh-heh, heh-heh-heh-heh! (*And he beats a little dance on the floor.*)

Costello (*replies with a dance, his fist through the ceiling again, dances a few steps with **John's Wife**; a sudden stitch in his side: he could be shamming, it's momentary*)   Hickle-ickle-ickle-ickle-ickle . . . (*Falsetto.*)

The others, in chorus, laugh at the antics and exchanges and, in turn, are silent.

Costello *and the **Stranger** are laughing together. A nod from **Costello** and they stop at the same moment. Their audience is puzzled.*

Costello   Hah?

Everyone laughs.

Costello (*sternly*)   Where (are) yeh bound for, me little man, your destination, a vicko?

Stranger   Ballindine-side, your worship.

Costello   Ballindine-side, Mayo, *a Thighearna* ('My Lord')! *Cunn ether iss syha soory*! (*Coinn iotair is saidhthe suaraighe.*)

Bina   Hounds of rage an' bitches of wickedness he's sayin' at you, mister!

Stranger   I know what he's sayin'. Heh-heh-heh-heh, heh-heh-heh-heh!

Costello   Ho-ho-ho-ho-ho-ho-ho!

Josie   Hinn-Mayo, God help us!

John   Josie, I'll – I'll put yeh out!

Costello   Here's the health of all Ireland save County Mayo, an' them that don't like it knows where they can go!

A reply from the **Stranger**, *drowned in the laughter and cheers of the others.*

Bina   Rise it, blasht yeh, lash it back at him!

John   Lave ('leave') him alone, p-pacin' himself – Isn't that what he's doin'?

Costello   Are yeh not insulted?

Stranger   Heh-heh-heh-heh-heh-heh-heh!

Martin John   Heh-heh-heh – What kind of laugh is that?

John   An' was siz-size of laugh a sis-stipulation, K-Kemple?

Costello *lets out a rumble of laughter,* **Stranger** *replies as before.*

Martin John   Half what you offered Tomás Rua, John, if Costello loses?

John *grimaces, brushes the offer of the bet away from him, but, at the same time, he's not ruling it out.*

John   J-Jasus, you're great, mister – He-he knows what he's d-doin', n-not like some of the friggin' p-plebs an' amadans I know! Your turn, Costello, or d'yeh want more drink on the house?

Costello *puts his glass on the counter for a refill. The whiskey that was taken away from the* **Stranger** *earlier is slipped back to him.* **Costello** *spits in his hands, spits on the floor.*

Costello (*sternly again*)   Who-what are yeh?

Josie   Hinnia – the Devil!

John   He's f-f-friggin' farmer!

Costello   A farmer?

Stranger   A goose one.

Costello   Wo-ho-ho, hickle-ickle-ickle-ickle!

John (*laughing*)   An' he's well able for yeh K-Costello!

Costello   An' yeh sold all your cargo?

Others laughing, **Stranger** *laughing.*

Stranger   An' yourself? – What're you in?

Costello (*mock seriousness*)   Oh now you're questioning me.

Martin John   Rabbits, sure!

Josie   Hull-hull-hull!

John   Josie! –

Stranger   Well, heh-heh-heh, heh-heh-heh, heh- heh-heh!

Costello   What's the cause of your laughter?

Stranger   Bunny rabbits: is *that* what you're in?!

Costello (*to* **Stranger**)   Not at all, me little man – I've a herd of Trinamanooses in Closh back the road.

Stranger (*mock innocent face also*)   Tame ones?

Costello   Tame ones, of a certainty, an' the finest breed for 'atin', sure.

Stranger   But for the townies, for city folks for 'atin'?

Their straight faces: whose face will break first?

Costello   Wo-ho-ho . . .! Give that man a drink!

Stranger   Heh-heh-heh-heh-heh-heh-heh!

Costello   Give that man a big drink!

Josie   Hinn – big drink! –

John   No! No! –

Costello   Wo-ho-ho . . .!

Stranger   Heh-heh-heh . . .!

The movement is to the bar. **John** *and his* **Wife** *serving drinks.*

John   Here, K-Costello, in spite of all your insults an' dirty talk. But that's the kind of man I am. Here, mister, an' that's your last till the contest's over. The man your k-contestin' again' would drink th-the Corrib dryan' he'd be only wettin' his lips with it. Th-the m-mouth an' the belly on him!

Brian *has been out to the yard and is returning, shaking rain off himself, going to the counter.*

John's Wife   Is it rainin' outside, Brian?

Brian   Kuh-hucktha, tis!

Martin John (*aside*)   Aisy on the tack, Séamus.

Costello (*dismissive*)   Haven't I it won? (*Catches* **John's Wife** *who is taking a drink to* **Stranger's Wife** *and dances with her.*) Rose, me thorny flower! (*Releases her and dances on his own in front of her: his virility.*)

Stranger   Heh-heh-heh-heh-heh-heh-heh!

Costello (*dances with* **Stranger**)   Heh-heh-heh-heh-heh-heh-heh, heh-heh-heh-heh-heh-heh-heh! – The poetry of John Mahony out courting his wife – (*Wiping his nose.*) 'There's shtars up that side an' there's shtars up that side'! . . . An' there was another man around here one time had this great taste for stealin' an' 'atin' other people's chickens –

Costello   Hickle-ickle-ickle-ickle!

Stranger   Heh-heh-heh-heh-heh-heh-heh!

Costello   An' he went to confession – Hickle-ickle-ickle –

Stranger   Heh-heh-heh –

Costello   An', 'Oh!' says he to the priest – 'Oh!' says he – Hickle-ickle-ickle! – 'Put as many prayers as you like on me for a penance, but don't ask me to fast' –

Stranger   Heh-heh-heh-heh –

Costello   Hickle-ickle-ickle – 'I'm a topper at the prayin' – Wo-ho-ho – Aw, Jesus, lads, I'm kilt!' ('killed') – 'I'm a topper at the prayin' –' Hickle-ickle-ickle – 'I'm a topper –' (*He's out of control.*)

Bina.   I'm a topper at the prayin' but I'm a hoor at the fasting!'

All laughing.

Anthony   Man, Costello! –

Josie   Man, hinnia! –

Martin John   Yeh have him, Séamus!

Costello   Aw, Jesus, lads, I'm – Wo-ho-ho . . .!

Martin John   Now who has it won?

John   Who-who-who has it won – Is it over yet? Mister!

Stranger   Heh-heh-heh-heh, heh-heh-heh-heh!

John   There ye a-are now!

Anthony   Come on, Costello!

Josie   Hih-hinnia!

Bina   Step it up, stranger, here's luck to yeh!

John   K-Costello's turn!

Costello   Gimme me glass – Hickle-ickle-ickle – hand me me pint – Wo-ho-ho . . .!

Stranger   Heh-heh-heh-heh-heh-heh-heh!

Costello *has his hand raised for silence.*

Costello   Point of information. An' just to show I'm not stoppin' for ulterior motivations, as the fella says, here's one: Wo-ho-ho-ho-ho-ho-ho-hickle-ickle-ickle-ickle . . .! Now, the question is, *how,* how is it to be indisputably decided who is the winner?

John   Oh, sh-sh-sh-sure . . . Hah?

Costello   Indisputably the winner.

Silence.

Stephen (*to the fire*)   'Tis a difficult question.

Stranger's Wife   He who laughs last!

Stranger is about to reprimand her but she is smiling at him softly and, without knowing why, he smiles back at her.

Costello   That's – that's what I thought.

Costello *spits on the floor. He paws at the spit with his boot. There is something of a lost bull about him.*

John (*quietly*)   Mister?

Stranger   Heh-heh-heh-heh-heh-heh-heh!

Stranger's Wife *laughs.*

John (*quietly*)   Costello's turn.

Costello   Wait'll I think of another . . . (story)

Martin John (*whispering*)   He's lost it.

Stephen   Oh yis!

Martin John   Come on, Séamus. (*Whispering.*) He never should have stopped.

Josie   Hih-hinnnnn!

Brian   Kuh-hucktha!

Martin John   Rise up the music – Give him a bar of a song, Bina!

John   She won't!

Bina   I won't!

John   N-n-no favouritism! He's bet!

Martin John   Come on, stranger, throw in a laugh to help him out!

Stranger   Heh-heh-heh –

John   No! L-laugh for l-l-l- Now, d'ye know!

Costello   Permission to go out the back!

John   No!

Costello   Oh? Did yeh sis-stipulate that we have to do it on the floor? (*And he looks at the* **Stranger** *for the his permission*).

Stranger   To be sure.

Costello   Thank you. (*To* **John**.) Now d'yeh know! (*Going out.*) Make way! I'm goin' out to shoot a few crows ('fart'). (*And he laughs going out the back door.*)

John   An' my little horse wuh-will be waitin' for yeh wh-when yeh get back!

And he laughs harshly after **Costello**. *He has taken a few steps after* **Costello**. *He nods to himself, he believes that* **Costello** *has had it.*

Martin John (*to himself*)   Aw Jasus, well if Costello isn't the right hoor! (*To* **Tomás Rua** *and* **Anthony**.) It's the signal. He's pullin', like he said he would. Now's your chance, Tomás, to try the Sheik (**John**) again . . .

Tomás Rua *goes to* **John**. *Through the following, we see the bet being struck and being entered in the book in sign language by Tomás Rua.*

The **Stranger's Wife** *is smiling:* **Stranger** *goes to her.*

Stranger   Ar, whist. Heh-heh-heh-heh! What's come over you?

She starts to laugh with him, quietly. They stop. Tears brim to her eyes. The misfortunes of a lifetime. She titters again. He laughs with her.

Stranger   It's rainin'. The thaw is set in. Shouldn't we be goin'?

Stranger's Wife *shakes her head, no.*

Stranger (*nods. Laughs quietly. His laugh, like hers, near tears*)   Ar, Mommo . . . But shouldn't we go?

Stranger's Wife   No . . . An' you have him bet.

She embraces him. They start to sway, as in a dance. It is like as if they have forgotten everyone around them in this moment.

Stranger   But 'twas only the comicalest notion that comes into a person's head.

Stranger's Wife   Whatever it was, you have him bet, you have them bet. We've been defeated in all else but this one thing we'll win.

They separate.

You'll get him with misfortunes.

Costello *has returned, he doesn't look well, genuinely, but he's trying to cover it.*

John   Now! The heh-hero is back!

Costello *striding to his pint. Murmers of encouragement from his supporters.*

Martin John (*aside to* **Costello**)   Well, if you aren't the greatest hoor in creation. (*In further compliment:*) Tomás Rua has his place bet on you.

Tomás Rua *is smiling at* **Costello***, his sickly daughter,* **Peggy***, beside him.*

Costello *hides his fear, drains his glass.*

Costello   Right! Are yeh ready? What's the topic?

Stranger   Misfortunes.

Costello   *What* misfortunes?!

Josie *goes 'Hih-hinnia',* **Peggy** *starts coughing,* **Tomás Rua** *puts his good arm around her, someone else limps in or out, the* **Stranger's Wife** *is laughing.*

The **Stranger** *laughs.*

Costello *taking off his jacket. His arms tangled in the sleeve, he can't get it off.* **John** *is laughing derisively at him, the others are laughing.* **Peggy** *is laughing.* **Costello**, *arms, jacket, a pullover caught in the jacket.*

John   K-clown, p-pleb, f-fool, he's bet!

Costello *sends his jacket and pullover into a corner and is making for* **John**. *He looks dangerous.*

Josie   Hinn – take – off – hinn – (your) trousers, Costello!

Suddenly **Costello** *has* **Josie** *by the throat. And now, for a moment, he can't think of a reason for his action.* **Josie** *can hardly breathe.*

Josie   Hnnnnn . . .!

Costello   Gimme the clock, I said!

Josie   Hnnnnn –

Costello   I'm not askin'!

Josie *gives him the clock (the usual cheap clock found on mantelpieces in country kitchens).* **Costello** *listens to it, shakes, etc.*

Costello   It's well mended alright. That clock now will go for a year without stoppin', standing on the mantelpiece, an' for two years more lyin' on its face. But the question is, can it fly?

A gasp from the others because his arm is aloft to throw the clock. Then the alarm goes off, startling him – 'Oh Jesus!' – making him drop the clock.

Josie, *who is on his knees, catches the clock and, a moment later,* **Bina** *takes it from him.*

Costello's *big laugh from the fright he has had, the others laughing with him, as is* **Josie**, *innocently, and as is the* **Stranger**.

Costello   Right! (*To* **Stranger**.) Are yeh sure yeh don't want to withdraw?

Stranger's Wife   There's no one talkin' about withdrawin' unless it's yourself.

Costello   . . . An' yeh sold all your cargo?

Stranger's Wife   Yeh said that!

Costello   An' an', did yeh sell the geese last year?

Stranger   No.

Costello   Oh?

Stranger   The fox got the lot of them – Heh-heh-heh-heh!

Costello   Wo-ho-ho-ho! An' the potatoes!

Stranger   Potatoes?

Anthony   How were they for yeh?

Brian   The damnable crop was in it this year.

Stranger   Oh, heh-heh, heh-heh-heh, heh-heh-heh!

Costello   Wet an' watery – Wo-ho-ho –

Stranger   Soapy an' sour – Heh-heh-heh –

Costello   But not blighted, d'yeh tell me? –

Stranger   No-no but scabby an' small.

Costello   Thin on the ground – Wo-ho-ho –

Stranger   Hard to dig – Heh-heh-heh –

Costello   Hard to wash, ladies, hard to boil, ladies? –

Bina   An' the divil t' ate!

All laughing; the contestants swapping laughs.

Brian   An' the hay, behell!

Costello *and* **Stranger**   Rotted!

Martin John   The bita oats – Jasus!

Brian   Lodged in the field!

Costello   An' the turf for the fire?!

Others   Still in the bog!

Bina   An' th'aul cow, mister?!

Stranger   Th'aul cow is still in it!

Martin John   An' the sheep! –

Costello   The staggers!

Bina   An' the chickens, the pip!

Brian   An' did we ever before see a summer like it?!

Stephen (*rising*)   Oh we did.

Brian   Kuh-hucktha, hah?

Stephen (*funereally, going out*)   Last winter.

(*He returns sometime later, shaking the rain off him.*)

Costello   An' your arm, Tomás Rua?!

Others   Lost to the thresher!

Josie   Eye-hinnia-eye! (*Pointing to* **Bina**.)

Costello   An' your eye, Bina?!

Bina   A hoor of a briar!

Stranger's Wife   An' the dead!

The momentum carries the laughter forward.

Costello   An' the dead – Wo-ho-ho! Me father, is it, you're referring to? Sure, he killed himself, sure: drowned himself in the barrel at the gable-end of the house.

Stranger   Heh-heh-heh-heh-heh-heh-heh!

Costello   'Twas a difficult feat. An' yourself, ma'am?

Stranger's Wife   I had nine sons –

Stranger   Heh-heh-heh-heh-heh-heh-heh!

Stranger's Wife   An' for the sake of an aul' ewe was stuck in the flood was how I lost Jimmy an' Michael.

Costello   Wo-ho-ho! – For the sake of an aul' ewe!

Stranger   Heh-heh-heh . . .!

Stranger's Wife   An' the nice wife Jimmy left behind, died, tryin' to give birth to the fourth child that was to be in it – Bate that!

Costello   Wo-ho-ho . . .! – Many's the one from here was lost to the water –

Stranger's Wife   An' Pat who was my first born –

Stranger   Heh-heh-heh . . .!

Stranger's Wife   Married the widdy against my wishes.

Costello   Wo-ho-ho . . .!

Stranger's Wife   The decline (TB) in that family! –

Others   The decline!

Stranger's Wife   An' when Pat came back for the two sheep (that) were his –

Stranger   Heh-heh-heh . . .!

Stranger's Wife   You'll not have them, I told him, and sent him back, lame, to his strap of a widdy –

Costello   Wo-ho-ho . . .!

Stranger's Wife   An' he was dead within a six months – Bate that!

Costello   Oh, sure – Hickle-ickle-ickle . . .!

Others   Man, Costello!

On, Costello!

Up Bochtán, on Bochtán!

Bochtán for ever!

Costello   Oh sure – Hickle-ickle-ickle-ickle . . .!

Stranger   Heh-heh-heh . . .!

Costello   Oh, sure, the decline – TB – lost to the water – tuberculosis – lost across the sea, in England –

Stranger's Wife   An' America! –

Stranger   An' America!

Stranger's Wife   One after the other!

Costello   One after the other! –

Stranger's Wife   Never to be heard of ever again! –

Costello   Wo-ho-ho, hickle-ickle-ickle . . .!

Stranger   Heh-heh-heh . . .!

Stranger's Wife   The unbaptised an' still-born in shoe-boxes planted

Costello   The unbaptised an' still-born –

Stranger's Wife   At the dead hour of night in unconsecrated ground –

Costello   In shoe-boxes planted – Many's the neighbour we went with – Hickle-ickle-ickle! – Didn't we Martin John?

Martin John   At the dead hour of night – Jasus! –

Costello   Treading softly the Lisheen –

Martin John   That field haunted by infants –

Costello   Too afeared to speak or to pray –

Stranger's Wife   Ye were fearful for yere ankles – Hih-hih-hih.

Stranger   Heh-heh-heh . . .!

Costello   Wo-ho-ho, hickle-ickle . . .!

Others cheering him.

Bina   Come on, mister, rise it! – Pneumonia, scarletina!

Martin John   Double pneumonia! –

Costello   Treble it! – Wo-ho-ho . . .!

John   F-f-fever, mister!

Bina   The chin-cough! –

Stranger   Dip'teria – Heh-heh-heh . . .!

Josie   Hinn-chicken bones! (*Choking on them.*) –

Brian   Pleurisy! –

Costello   Meningitis! – Hickle-ickle . . .!

Stranger's Wife   Per'tonitis! –

Brian   The 'looseness' –

Stranger   Heh-heh-heh-heh-heh-heh . . .!

Costello   Dysentery, malaria, a stroke! – Hickle-ickle . . .

Josie   Hinnia-chicken bones!

Stranger's Wife (*laughing*)   Hih-hih-hih!

Stranger   Heh-heh-heh . . .!

Costello   Wo-ho-ho, hickle-ickle . . .

Costello   The still-born an' forlorn! – Wo-ho-ho . . .!

Stranger   The lonely an' bereaved! – Heh-heh-heh . . .!

Costello   Half-starved, half-demented! – Hickle-ickle . . .!

Others   Those lost to America!

Arms lost to the thresher!

Suicide an' bad weather!

Blighted crops!

Bad harvests!

Bad markets!

How to keep the one foot in front of the other!

Per'tonitis!

An' yellow fever, black an' scarlet!

Chicken-bones!

Briars to take out your eyes!

Or to bate the children with!

Put *smacht* ('manners') on them when there's nought for their bellies!

Miadh, misfortunes!

Costello   And there's more maybe to come!

Stranger's Wife (*to the heavens*)   Send us more!

Others   Send them!

Stranger   We're waitin'!

Costello   We are!

Others   We are!

Stranger's Wife   For anything else to come, or might care to come!

Costello (*like the others, shouting at the heavens*)   Send us your best!

All shouting, their heads thrown back in defiant laughter – except **John**. *Fists are puncturing the ceiling, feet stamping the floor.*

John   Are ye t-t-temptin' the Almighty? God's goodness? Stand back, let the k-contest continue! No-no-no-no more drink till the contest is decided. D'ye know now!

An order is gradually achieved. Now we see **Costello**, *doubled-up, straightening-up, loosening his buckle, opening down his shirts, holding his sides, staggering about. He is now, all the time, in the upper register – 'Hickle-ickle'. He cannot stop it.*

The **Stranger**, *too, is holding his sides and doubling-up occasionally. But there is a stillness coming over him, a concern and a fear as he watches* **Costello** *changing colour.*

Costello   Hickle-ickle-ickle-ickle . . .!

Stranger   Heh-heh-heh-heh-heh-heh!

Costello   Hickle-ickle-ickle-ickle . . .!

Others   Man, Costello! Man, Séamus!

Bina   More power to yeh, stranger!

John   Now, mister, again!

Stranger   Heh-heh-heh-heh-heh-heh-heh!

Costello   Aw Jasus, lads – (*A fit of coughing.*)

John   N-now, mister, again!

Stranger   Heh-heh-heh-heh-heh-heh-heh!

Costello   Hickle-ickle-ickle-ickle – Aw Jays, lads, I'm – Hickle-ickle-ickle-ickle!

John   Now, m-mister, again!

Stranger   Heh-heh-heh-heh-heh-heh-heh!

Costello   Aw Jays lads, I'm dyin' – Hickle-ickle-ickle-ickle! Aw Jays, lads, I'm – Hickle-ickle-ickle-ickle!

John   Now, m-mister, again!

Stranger   Heh-heh-heh-heh-heh-heh-heh!

Costello   Hickle-ickle-ickle-ickle – (*His hand up to call a stop, but he can barely raise his arms.*)

Martin John   Lave (*leave*) the ceiling to us, Séamus!

(*Punching the ceiling, as is* **Anthony**.)

Martin John   On-on, Costello!

Tomás Rua. Come on, Costello!

John   M-mister! –

Bina   Stranger!

Stranger   Heh-heh-heh-heh . . . heh-heh-heh!

Costello   Aw, Jays, lads, I'm – Hickle-ickle-ickle –

He is falling over himself, occasionally leaning on someone for support. Every time, he is pushed back into the 'arena'.

John   N-now, mister, in at him again!

Costello   An' the rabbits, lads – Hickle-ickle- ickle-ickle!

Bina   Answer him, stranger!

John   R-r-reply, mister!

Costello   I didn't sell e'er the one of them but threwn them comin' home for fun agin' Patch Curran's door! Hickle-ickle-ickle . . .!

Others   Yahoo!

Costello, you have him!

On Bochtán!

Up Bochtán!

Bochtán for ever!

Stranger   Heh-heh-heh! (*Quietly; the two little smiles on the corners of his mouth.*)

Bina   Blasht yeh, stranger, louder!

Stranger (*suddenly shouts*)   Stop! Costello's the winner!

Stranger's Wife   He's nat ('not'), he's nat, he's nat, he's nat!

John   N-not, f-false!

Bina   He's not!

Costello *and the* **Stranger** *are now together in the centre of the floor,* **Costello** *supporting himself on the* **Stranger***'s shoulders.*

Stranger   Stop, man, stop.

Costello   Hickle-ickle-ickle – I can't – hickle-ickle . . .!

Stranger   Heh-heh-heh-heh-heh-heh-heh!

Bina   God bless yeh, stranger!

John   N-n-now! Now!

Stranger   Costello's the winner!

Costello   Hickle-ickle-ickle-ickle . . .!

Stranger   Heh-heh-heh-heh-heh – Stand up straight, your full height, I'll not laugh anymore.

Costello *is embracing the* **Stranger** *– they are like two people in a slow dance.* **Costello**'s *'hickle-ickle' continues but he now appears to be whispering to the* **Stranger**. *The* **Stranger** *appears to nod to what is being whispered; he appears to be close to tears.*

Costello's *laughter peters out.*

Stranger   Heh-heh-heh-heh-heh-heh-heh!

The two of them collapse on the floor, **Costello**, *face down, across the* **Stranger**'s *legs, the* **Stranger** *sitting up.*

The noise subsides to silence.

John   Ih-ih-ih-is he . . . is he?

Josie (*quietly*)   Hinnnnnn! (*Crouches down, shakes* **Costello**'s *foot.*) Hinnnnnn . . .?

John   G-g-go for the priest, one of ye. L-last laugh. The book h-has to stand.

Josie *is crying at death and becoming excited: the* **Stranger** *is the Devil, the* **Stranger's Wife** *is the Devil's wife: the boots have to be taken off the* **Stranger** *to prove it, i.e. that the* **Stranger** *has hooves, not feet.*

Josie   Hinn-devil, Hinn-devil's wife – Hinn-boots off –

John   Come on, Josie, a mac –

Josie *is tugging at the* **Stranger**'*s boots and swiping at the* **Stranger**. *The* **Stranger** *is trying to get up. The others are pressing forward: confused, becoming wild-eyed, beginning to make low, angry sounds.* **John**, *with his book, pulling* **Josie** *back.*

Josie   Hinn-boots? Till we see if he has feet or no in them! –

John   G-go, mister – Sis-sis-stop, Josie –

One of **Josie**'*s swings sends the book flying out of* **John**'*s hands.* **John** *falls back against the others, one of his arms catching someone in the mouth, the other catching* **Bina**. *Someone else catches someone else.* **John**, *coming forward to retrieve his book, is sent sprawling over* **Josie** *and* **Costello** *by* **Martin John** . . . *Mayhem. Clamouring.* **Stranger** *and his* **Wife** *trying to defend themselves, getting out the door. The melee goes out the door. Only the* **Child** *remains, looking at the prone body of* **Costello**.

Voices outside:

Voices   Hinnia – Devil! Go, yeh Devil yeh! An' bad luck to ye! Skelong!

Stranger's Wife's Voice   An' 'tis glad we are to be goin' from the rogues and thieves that parade Bochtán an' the villainy of Galway!

Voices   Pull them down off the cart!

Jasus, d'ye hear them!

Give him the kickin'!

That's it, welt him!

L-let them go, let them off!

Ye unholy couple!

Skelong, skelong!

An' never come back!

Hounds of rage, bitches of wickedness!

Bad luck to ye!

The horse and cart moving off: as it fades. During the last, the **Child** *puts his fingers in his mouth:* **Costello** *stirs. The* **Child** *runs to his parents who are coming in with the others.* **Costello** *is at death's door but he isn't dead.*

Martin John   Aw, Jasus, no, John, nothing stands!

Bina   The book stands!

Martin John   Sure all must be declared null an' void: a man is dead.

John   An'-an' the h-heavens be his bed! But huh-who laughed last? The b-book stands. Now d'ye know.

The **Child** *finally draws their attention to* **Costello** *who has raised himself up a little.*

Costello   Wo-ho-ho-ho-ho-ho-ho . . .!

Silence.

Josie   Hih-hinn?

Stephen   Oh yis!

Brian   Kuh-huckta!

Martin John   The book stands. Yeh owe us ten pounds. Yeh owe Tomás Rua a lot more.

Bina   An' I lost nothin'. Fifteen pounds out of what yeh owe Costello for me cow.

Josie   Hinnia-one-penny – ha'penny.

John   J-Jasus, me head! J-Jasus, Costello, an' th-the priest comin' to send you off!

They put **Costello** *in a chair.*

Costello   I'm goin' (*dying*). You'll give the hundred pounds to me mother.

John   'T-'t'll be honoured, 't'll be honoured.

Costello   Wo-ho-ho! An' that's the last laugh.

John   An'-an' that'll be honoured too, k-cause if I ever hear as much as a-a – (*giggle*) – in here ever again, I'll – I'll – I'll!

Costello   I always had a wish to see a bit of me own wake. Let ye begin it till I see what it's like.

The music starts up. Hands are raised: people are buying rounds of drink. The wake is lively. **Josie** *is bringing a pint to* **Costello** *but his head has fallen to one side. He's dead.* **Josie** *sits on the floor beside* **Costello**'s *chair.*